Poverty, Celibacy, and Obedience

Diarmuid O'Murchu

Poverty, Celibacy, and Obedience

A RADICAL OPTION FOR LIFE

A Crossroad Book
The Crossroad Publishing Company
New York

The artwork on the cover and the title page is by Lucinda Naylor.

The Crossroad Publishing Company
370 Lexington Avenue, New York, NY 10017

Printed in the United States of America

Library of Congress Cataloging-in-Publication Data

   O'Murchu, Diarmuid.
  Poverty, celibacy, and obedience : a radical option for life /
    Diarmuid O'Murchu.
   p. cm.
  Includes bibliographical references (p.).
  ISBN 0-8245-1473-4 (pbk.)
  1. Evangelical counsels. 2. Ahiṃsā.   I. Title.
BX2435.O33 1999
255–dc21   98-41199

3   4   5   6   7   8   9   10   03   02   01   00   99

Contents

Introduction

This book is about the three vows of the monastic and religious life, traditionally known as poverty, celibacy (chastity), and obedience. In our Western Christian tradition, we tend to associate the vows with a life of special commitment and dedication to God. Although the strict enclosure of ages past no longer prevails, living the vowed life still denotes separation from the world in order to be more fully committed to following Christ and living the spiritual life in a unique way.

Consequently, aligning the vows with the notion of nonviolence will surprise many and, perhaps, confuse some. Violence is perceived to be very much a secular issue, instigated by those who are preoccupied with the affairs of the world. And this misperception leads to an even more misplaced one: the remedies to the violence of our world are perceived to be the primary responsibility of those who deal with the affairs of the world and not for those called to serve Christ in the vowed life.

Already we are immersed in one of the primary causes of violence — all violence — namely, dualistic thinking, the human compulsion to divide everything into adversarial opposites. So much of our daily lives is governed by dualistic thought and modeling! We presume that it has always been that way, that that is the way God intended life to be. We need to confront our own delusions — including those that have bedeviled the monastic and religious life for many centuries. It is we humans who invented dualisms and not God. Out of our insatiable desire to divide and conquer we juxtaposed reality into conflicting pairs of opposites. And over time — an estimated ten thousand years — we presumed that this is how life should be and that this is how God wanted it to be.

1

The dualistic mind-set is also a distinctly Western phenomenon. Peoples of the East have a much deeper appreciation of
how things connect rather than divide. The concept of nonviolence itself (*ahimsa*) is of Eastern origin and never seems
to have been integrated into Western spirituality as it has
been in the East.

Complementarity rather than dualistic opposition characterizes the spiritual cultures of Eastern peoples. Not surprisingly, therefore, the values of the vowed life as lived out
in the great Eastern traditions of Hinduism, Buddhism, and
Jainism are much more transparent in terms of harmony and
integration than our Western approach. We have much to
learn from the Eastern experience.

Our willingness to dialogue with the East and learn from
its experience itself requires a conversion if we are to move
beyond the East vs. West dualism and especially the ideological division between Christian and non-Christian per-
spectives. In this age of multifaith dialogue it is baffling and,
for me, deeply disappointing, to see how many books on the
monastic or religious life do not make even a single reference
to the great Eastern experience. Our intellectual and spiritual
insularism itself feeds the culture of division and violence.

However, this book is not motivated simply by a desire for multifaith dialogue, valuable though that may be
in itself. I also want to rescue the vowed life from the religious minimalism that is choking it to death. I want to
transcend the centuries of legalistic and devotional modeling
that portrayed the vows as the means toward perfection that
guaranteed salvation in a life hereafter.

I want to reclaim what I believe is a much deeper and
more authentic tradition in which the vowed life engages
with the archetypal values[1] that govern our earthly, personal,
and interpersonal lives. It is these global and planetary —
as well as personal and interpersonal — dimensions of the
vowed life that surface afresh under the rubric of nonviolence, itself a key aspect for the unfolding spirituality and
theology for our time.

My envisaged readership are those called to the vowed life in any of the major faith traditions. My hope is that this will include the increasing numbers of lay people who identify with our values and our vision and increasingly work with us in close collaboration. The insights of this book, while applied directly to those called to the vowed life, are clearly not reserved to that special group. They have a universal application and, indeed, an urgent one in a world held to ransom by so much mindless and barbaric violence.

The book is not about making peace in a new way, nor is it merely about abandoning violence. Its invitation is to what the Christian gospel calls the "fulness of life" (John 10:10), or what St. Paul has in mind in the unqualified "Yes" to life (2 Cor. 1:19). The way of nonviolence is a radical option *for* life; so, too, is the commitment to the vowed life, at least in theory. It is the gap between the ideal and the real that this book attempts to bridge in a new way. Hopefully, the fresh challenge will evoke a new enthusiasm for life, in religious and in lay people alike.

CHAPTER ONE

Nonviolence: The Way to Wholeness

*Religion has claimed to love life while pursuing death —
and has kept the rules in place by terror.*

— ROBIN MORGAN

*If I may say so without arrogance, my message and my
methods are indeed, in their essentials, for the whole
world. I believe myself to be a revolutionary, a nonviolent revolutionary. I am aspiring for a new order of
things that will astonish the world.*

— MAHATMA GANDHI

In the present century alone over a hundred million people
have perished in warfare. An estimated one billion people
have died from starvation and malnutrition. As many again
have been subjected to torture and incarceration sometimes
for several decades. Add to all that the animals, fishes, and
other species we slaughter on a daily basis either for human
consumption or for some other purpose. And let's not forget
the stripping of the tropical forests, the pollution of air and
water and the erosion of tons of topsoil — all for economic
exploitation. One can be left in little doubt that we live in a
world saturated in violence.

Far more disturbing is the realization that it is we humans, and not any other secular or sacred force, who cause
and inflict well over 90 percent of that violence. We are the
most barbaric life form inhabiting Planet Earth and, it would
seem, the whole cosmos. Theorists ranging from philoso-

phers to anthropologists to psychologists have long believed that aggression is built into the very make-up of our humanity, and they accumulate a great deal of evidence to verify this fact. Only in the past ten years have we begun to see a major flaw in the argument: all the evidence is taken from the past ten thousand years.

Prior to that time we assume that things were much the same, and in all probability much worse. But a growing body of anthropological and archaeological research suggest the very opposite. Our ancient ancestors seem to be for the greater part creatures who lived in relative peace and harmony, with one another, with other life forms, and with Planet Earth (see the pioneering work of Eisler 1987). The Agricultural Revolution changed all that as we vied and competed for the acquisition and use of land. We shifted from being a (largely) nonviolent to an extremely violent species. And now the violence is coming home to roost. Our own destructibility is haunting us with the looming demise of our own extinction. Yes, it is no exaggeration: things have gotten drastically out of hand, and it will take something truly miraculous if we are to be saved from our own barbarity — a rather grim state of affairs that I elucidate in a previous work (O'Murchu 1997b, 141–56).

An Ancient Ideal

It is against this background that we need to review the rising consciousness around nonviolence that has characterized the present century particularly. The concept is not new. Many ancient Vedic texts enunciate and advocate this strategy. Hinduism, Buddhism, and particularly Jainism (see Dundas 1992; Jaini 1979) make nonviolence a central tenet of their belief systems. Scholars such as Ferguson (1975) and Fuller (1978) argue that Jesus totally endorsed the nonviolent approach, launching early Christianity as a radically pacifist movement until it became the official religion of the empire early in the fourth century. Then there was a sudden and tragic reversal of values and the collusion became so powerful that doctors of the church such as St. Augustine were lured into creating the theory of a "just war." In fact the principle was so widely abused that St. Thomas Aquinas in the thirteenth century affirmed that war is *always* sinful, even if it is occasionally waged for a just cause.

More important, however, and much more difficult to unravel are the dominant archetypes of the patriarchal worldview in which early Christianity became embedded. I am referring to two developments in particular: the valorization of the warrior (and of war) in the Indo-European religious culture, often dated to the fifth century B.C.E. and classically exposed by Dumezil (1956, 1970); second, the exoneration of the mythic hero who became the prototype of all great spiritual ascetics. Both these metaphors require and are validated by a patriarchal God-image as conqueror, ruler, and battle-winner supreme. It is no exaggeration to suggest, as Morgan (1989) does quite overtly, that religion instigates a culture of terrorism.

Over the centuries, the collusion of church and state became so enmeshed that it took a range of subversive movements to keep alive the pacifist and nonviolent vision. Among the better known were the Waldensians in the twelfth century, the Lollards, Hussites, and Taborites in the fifteenth, the Mennonites in the sixteenth, and, perhaps best known of all, the Quakers in the seventeenth. But it is in the twentieth century especially that we are reclaiming this ancient and unrelenting ideal. And nobody has embodied it more coherently and creatively than the great Mahatma Gandhi (1869–1948).

Gandhi was clearly influenced by his Indian Hindu and Jain culture. Adopting the Sanskrit notion of *ahimsa* (literally, noninjury), Gandhi developed his theory of passive resistance to activate a new quality of truth (*satyagraha*, or truth-force) across the entire spectrum of personal, interpersonal, social, and political relationships. And central to

Gandhi's vision was belief in God, the ultimate source and foundation of all truth.

In the spiritual tradition of the East, *ahimsa* is often presented as a means of expediting the process of rebirth. By refraining from causing harm or damage to other creatures or to nature in its many aspects, devotees believe they are helping to diminish the impact of negative *karma* and thus contributing to their own eventual liberation into a state of ultimate bliss (*nirvana*). This interpretation closely resembles the traditional emphasis in Western spirituality on the priority of individual salvation and the conviction that salvation is fully attainable only outside and beyond this earthly realm.

Ahimsa, *a Divine Attribute*

Gandhi stretched this limited vision to radically new horizons. *Ahimsa* is depicted not so much as a spiritual strategy to be adopted by human beings, but rather as a central aspect of God's own life and of God's concern for the world. It is primarily a divine attribute, a central aspect of the divine *shalom* (peace), whereby we humans are invited to live and work harmoniously and constructively to advance the fullness and wholeness of life that every major religion claims as its central teaching (see the informed study by Tähtinen 1976).

It is in order to know God's wishes more clearly and follow them more fully that Gandhi goes on to advocate an ascetical code of conduct. Those committed to a nonviolent way must seek in their own life the conditions of inner peace and harmony: purity of heart and intention, nonattachment to earthly possessions, care and self-discipline in the use of food, restraint and gentleness in sexual matters, peaceful relations with all creatures. People must not seek exclusive power or possession over any human or earthly realities, since all things are gifted to us by God. By the same token, coercion and intimidation are deemed to be violent and therefore to be abhorred (see Chapple 1993).

Many of the great mystics down through the ages and across all the cultures of humankind have adopted similar ideals and aspirations. Where Gandhi, and more recently Martin Luther King, differs is in advocating social and political structures that will safeguard and augment these values and aspirations. In this regard Gandhi far exceeds the traditional spirituality of both East and West.

It is not a question of purifying ourselves in the here-and-now so that we can eventually escape this violent, sinful world for the peace and harmony that belong to the life here-after. Rather the divine and human challenge is portrayed as a radical engagement in the here and now, political as well as spiritual, to bring about that divine transformation that God intends for our world and its peoples.

Nonviolence is the handmaid of true biblical justice, the righteousness that seeks to abolish all oppression and ex-ploitation so that people can enjoy the freedom of the children of God. This involves the risky and unprecedented initiative of seeking reconciliation even with one's oppressor. Nonviolence also underpins the radically new vision of Jesus proclaimed in the *Basileia* (the Kingdom of God), God's own original reign at the heart of creation characterized by justice, love, peace, and liberation.[2]

The history of Christendom, in conjunction with many of the great religions, exhibits some tragic and terrible devia-tions from the way of peace and nonviolence. The Hebrew Scriptures, despite what scholars perceive to be the central role of the covenant, provide a long and laborious litany of butchery, barbarity, and oppression. So many wars and treaties of the past two thousand years were fought and forged with the church frequently colluding in torture and subjugation. The Islamic jihad stands as a grim and sinis-ter reminder of how we twist and distort our spiritual vision into something blasphemous and outrageous.

And the great Eastern religions, home to so much cre-

ative vision and thought around the notion of nonviolence
(*ahimsa*), also stand knee-deep in bloodshed and oppression.
Indeed on the Indian subcontinent, the spirituality of nonviolence rarely has impacted upon the appalling poverty and
deprivation, exacerbated by an oppressive caste system, that
the Indian people have had to endure for so long.

The Power of Nonviolent Politics

As with many of the great and central values of humankind, the retrieval of these values happens outside rather
than within the religious institutions. The people themselves
muster up their own creative ways to reclaim that which is
in danger of being submerged forever. This universal will-
to-meaning is a central element in the emerging theology
of religious life. It is manifest particularly in the "liminality," the option for the cutting-edge, which characterizes the
vowed life in a unique way.[3] I'll return to this topic later in
the present chapter.

Miller (1972, 224–365) offers several examples of nonviolence at work in resolving political and social tensions
over the past two hundred years. Nonviolent general strikes
led to the overthrow of seven Latin American dictators in
the course of this century. Throughout the 1980s, the solidarity movement in Poland transformed the entire political
landscape. The power of the people's resistance brought an
end to the Marcos dictatorship in the Philippines in 1986.

Shortly thereafter, we witnessed the transforming impact
of people's nonviolent power in the dismantling of the Berlin
Wall and the collapse of communist power in the Eastern
bloc. And finally, against heavy odds, not a drop of blood
was shed as the apartheid regime in South Africa ended and
the country elected its first democratic government.

These are some of the recent outstanding achievements
of nonviolent politics. What is not apparent but is much
more significant (in my opinion) is the less obvious, often

hidden — even subverted — pacifist action that undergirds shifts in consciousness that ultimately bring about the most profound changes of all. Here I allude to the work of movements like the Campaign for Nuclear Disarmament (CND) and Greenpeace. Were it not for the long, arduous, and nonviolent protests of a group like CND over some twenty years, I believe we would not have seen the dramatic change of heart that took place in 1986 that marked the beginning of the end of the Cold War. By the same token, the challenge to address so many of the urgent ecological and environmental questions of our time has been brought about largely through the shift in global consciousness made possible by organizations such as Friends of the Earth, Worldwatch, and particularly Greenpeace.

Despite the fact that warfare is still rampant in our world and destructive violence is widespread, people of the twentieth and twenty-first centuries yearn for peace, and for peaceful means to resolve difficulties, to a degree rarely known over many thousands of years. In part, this desire is fueled by the alarming increase in domestic and personal violence in recent decades and also in part because more and more people are becoming disillusioned with mainstream governments and don't trust them to be able to deliver peaceful and harmonious solutions on any issue of major concern. Added to all that, however, is a distinctive change of consciousness, more transparent to the ideals and aspirations of pacifism and more convinced than ever that nonviolent means is the only true path to lasting peace and progress.

The Monastic Heritage

Mahatma Gandhi inherited his nonviolent vision not so much from a broad religious tradition but more specifically from the living contemporary witness of monks and nuns on the Indian subcontinent. Although the Jain, Hindu, and Buddhist faiths encourage everybody to adopt the values of the nonviolent way, it is those called to the monastic life who live them out in the most concrete and systematic manner.

The Great Vows (Mahavrata) of Jainism seek to ensure that the monastic devotee causes not the slightest damage or harm to any living organism. This is particularly apparent in the attention given to food. Vegetarianism is strictly adopted with the added requirement that one uses only those vegetables and fruits that have reached their full growth potential. As far as possible every living organism is to be allowed to live out its full life cycle.

Stories abound on the idiosyncrasies that accompany these noble expectations. Some devotees cover their faces so that they don't breathe in tiny creatures of the air and in that way kill them; others brush the pathway as they walk to ensure that they do not step on any living organism. In highlighting these examples we are in danger of trivializing the deeper meaning. The ultimate intention is not one of preserving life for its own sake; rather God, the source of all life, requires us to behave in this way.

Ahimsa is much more an inner disposition of heart than an external set of behaviors. It is primarily a celebration of the prodigious fertility of God and of the primacy of God's creativity and care for everything that exists. It requires of the devotee not merely a sense of respect for all God's creation but an inner discipline, an asceticism, that inculcates a state of mindfulness, a deep contemplative attentiveness to the sacredness and uniqueness of every living organism. This sense of attentiveness requires the monks and nuns to be deeply aware of their own attitudes and tendencies and to acquire appropriate self-discipline in thought and action to become authentic witnesses to nonviolent living.

Moderation and restraint are two key qualities. The monastic person strives to live with great simplicity, possessing only the essentials to live and survive. Popular works often portray this way of life as one of destitution and deprivation. In fact, when authentically lived, it does not breed coldness or indifference to the surrounding culture, but a deep sense of care and compassion.

Monastic persons feel at one with those condemned to suffering and marginalization in the world, the victims of violence and oppression. They may not be able to change the plight of the poor and the suffering, but they do render an invaluable service of naming the causes of that suffering, standing in prayerful solidarity with the victims of oppression and challenging the conventional and often superficial perceptions people adopt in trying to understand the world of their day.

Although monastic persons are separated from the world, they are often deeply attuned to what's going on there and, in largely unexplained and paradoxical ways, exert an influence for good. One thinks of the influence of people like Thomas Merton and Bede Griffiths and many others like them in our world today. What we have probably underestimated in the past, and are now challenged to consider anew, is the power of the monastic presence (the community) to influence and affect the surrounding culture. In both her writings and her ministries, Joan Chittister addresses this challenge with unique vision and vitality (see especially Chittister 1995).

Reinterpreting the Vows

Monastic and religious life as lived the world over adopts a set of solemn promises, known as rules or vows. In the West, we have traditionally named these as poverty, chastity, and obedience (and in some cases a vow of stability). In all the traditions, the vows tend to be explored and explained in ascetical, world-denouncing terms. They are portrayed as laws whose strict observance will protect you from the evils of the world and ensure that you attain eternal bliss in the afterlife. By pursuing the monastic ideal, sanctity became synonymous with heroism, and the holiness of the monastery became the ideal which all should strive to emulate.

Not surprisingly, we have — in all the religions of the world — a two-tier understanding of holiness. The monastic life is considered to be the better and the holier and, consequently, the lay way of life is deemed to be inferior and imperfect. Despite genuine effort over the past thirty years to change this dualistic and discriminatory distinction, the old division still looms large and seriously inhibits a more integrated spirituality for monk and lay person alike.

In previous works (O'Murchu 1991, 1995), I have examined the deeper significance of the vowed life as a liminal, prophetic calling, lived out by a small group on behalf of all God's people. In this context the vows are concerned primarily with values and not with laws. Our human preoccupation with legislating for every eventuality in human life is a relatively recent development in our evolutionary history as a human species. It is not easily unraveled, tied up as it is with complex cultural and religious dynamics. Culturally, we still live in the shadow of ten thousand years of patriarchy, the male-dominated desire to control and subdue every facet of human and planetary life, often exerted through brutal force, and in more recent times by laws to cover every conceivable outcome of human behavior.

The rise of formal religion needs to be understood and interpreted within this broad frame of reference. Religion validated (or rather was construed to validate) the values of the dominant patriarchal culture. Even to this day, male control predominates in all the major religions. The history of the vowed life in the various creeds provides extensive coverage of great male achievements and relatively little of the female contribution, although in some cases (e.g., Christianity) females have always outnumbered the males. The history of religious life, like so much sacred history, is soaking in the stench of patriarchal oppression. And although it can record outstanding achievements of holiness and service to humanity, it is not and must not be considered beyond the critique which the pursuit of truth and gospel transparency requires of us all today.

The notion of reinterpreting the vows against the background of nonviolence is not as original as it sounds. As already indicated, it has a long history in the great Eastern traditions of the vowed life (which sadly, Western scholars rarely attend to). More importantly, it is an approach that enables and empowers us to get in touch with those deeper spiritual values that predate the patriarchal manipulation of spirituality.

It helps to reconnect us with those long subverted traditions of holiness that belong to prepatriarchal times when the shaman served as prototype for the vowed way of life.[4] In this ancient context, it seems that values and not laws were paramount. And all indications are that the values were very similar to those enunciated by Jesus in proclaiming the *Basileia* as the basic requirement for authentic Christian living.

In pursuing the meaning of the vows in the context of nonviolence, we are not merely updating their relevance for our own time, but, more importantly, we are reviving ancient and deeper meanings of the monastic and religious life itself. By focusing on the value orientation of the vows, we are invited to reclaim the significance of the vowed life for all God's people and not merely for those called to live that life. We are invited to forego the "hierarchical" ordering whereby those perceived to be holier and better must serve as models for the rest of us, an ordering that belongs to human manipulation rather than divine initiative. We are asked to reclaim the ancient wisdom and practice whereby we humans create liminal groups and spaces in which we can enculturate those deeper values that forever burn in our hearts. Central to such values is the yearning to live harmoniously and creatively with ourselves, with others, with nature, and with our God.

Those called to live the vowed life are the recipients of a vocation that belongs to *all* God's people, even to those who have no explicit faith in God. The call is special in the sense that those called are invited to live out more deeply the values that all people yearn for. The values, however, are not uniquely monastic ones, but those that all people aspire to from within their God-given spiritual endowment.

The vows, therefore, are conglomerates of values, all of which relate to the human search for meaning. Poverty is not about sacrificing material goods but about exercising stewardship over the goods of creation according to the equality and integrity of the gospel. Chastity is not about abstinence from sexual thoughts and acts but about engaging with the daily struggle and challenge of authentic sexual and relational growth. Obedience is not about submitting our will to a higher authority (why then did God give us a will in the first place?) but about exploring and proffering ever new ways to engage responsibly, collaboratively, and creatively with the issues of power and powerlessness that we encounter in daily life. The engagement with values, and not the observance of laws, is what the vowed life entails in its primary and pristine meaning.

In emphasizing values I do not wish to dismiss laws as being totally unnecessary. The purpose of law — all law — is to protect freedom. That in itself is a value we have largely lost sight of. In a world where, on the one hand, millions flout the law and, on the other, legalism and litigation is rampant — while those who administer law are among the wealthiest people in the world — a lot of serious questions beg serious answers. Are we becoming so reliant on law that we are in danger of turning both our laws and our legislators into yet another set of false gods? At the end of the day it is not laws but values that touch the depth of our human hearts.

Dealing with Liminal Questions

The reader may wonder why a book on the vowed life raises such complex questions that seem to belong to the affairs of the world rather than the reality of God. This is where we need to restate, briefly, the theology of religious life that underpins this new understanding of the vows, a theology I develop at length in two previous books (O'Murchu 1991, 1995).

The call to the vowed life is universal in nature and predates, historically and culturally, all the major religions known to humankind. Religious life needs neither formal religion nor the Christian Church to validate its existence. Although essentially spiritual in nature and incapable of comprehension or explanation apart from its spiritual raison d'être, it does not require formal religion either for its existence or development.

Religious life belongs to God and to people. It arises from those deep spiritual yearnings of the human heart as people strive to articulate, explicate, and negotiate their key values. The values themselves do not change from one age to the next; in a sense they are permanent and enduring. How we enculturate those values, how we translate them into personal, interpersonal, social, and political action is a human dynamic from within which people invent "liminal movements" to assist them in grounding and living out their God-given value orientation. A great deal of this process happens subconsciously; we are not consciously aware of what we are doing, because other forces — divine, cosmic, and planetary — are all involved in this process.

In Plato's *Republic,* his seminal rendition on the meaning of politics (probably written around 365 B.C.E.), we read about the small utopian group whose task it was to be the cutting-edge of political life, thus guaranteeing justice and meaning for the entire political community. Edwards (1976, 372) comments:

> The famous Platonic guardians were to be brought into the world in accordance with premeditated principles of eugenics and were not to know who their parents were. They were to live in conditions of complete communism and poverty, without privacy and outside the family; both men and women were to spend their whole lives

at the service of the polis and undergo thirty years of education.... Although it is implied that the guardians would be a small minority of the whole population, and that their undisturbed rulership would ensure justice, their relationship with the other two elements in the polis, the soldiery and the consumers...is never specified. These divisions of the polis are presented as divisions of the soul; indeed, the polis is the soul writ large. In so far as there is a positive political doctrine in this most famous of all works of political philosophy, it seems to be hypothetical — if the polis-soul could be constructed in this way, then all problems would be solved.

The term "liminality" was coined by Arnold Van Gennep in 1909 and therefore unknown in Plato's time, but Plato seems to have been aware of its immemorial significance and expresses its meaning in vivid and practical terms. It is also worthy of note that Plato envisioned politics as the sphere in which this most sublime of spiritual aspirations would be lived out. I'll return to this topic in subsequent chapters. The vocation to religious life is, above all else, a liminal calling, a threshold experience, to those places apart where we are invited to provide a mirror-image in which the people can see reflected their own searchings, struggles, and hopes for a more meaningful existence. It is the people (or, more accurately, God working through the people) that create the liminal spaces. And those called apart are accountable first and foremost to the people (what Plato calls the *polis*), and not to the church or to any formal religious system.

It is unfortunate that religious life today is so closely identified with formal religion. It confuses many issues but, most fundamentally, the meaning of the vowed life as a cultural, global movement. It also spiritualizes monastic and religious life to a degree that seriously undermines its liminal potential. The vowed life was never intended to be secluded in monasteries or convents and, ironically, for the greater part of its existence it has not been. Despite all the attempts at enclosure and seclusion (comprehensively reviewed by Mc-Namara 1996), the liminal people touch the hearts and lives of God's people and no doubt will continue to do so in the future.

The major crisis facing the vowed life today is that it has largely lost touch with its capacity to serve in a liminal capacity. It has been heavily domesticated and excessively institutionalized, not merely in religious (ecclesiastical) terms but also because it has overidentified with the conventional behaviors of secular life. Religious tend to work and minister in institutions and systems sponsored by state or church, sometimes by both. Such involvement seriously hinders the ability to act in a liminal and prophetic way.

The liminality is not threatened. The people will ensure that there will always be liminal places and liminal people to shake up our staid institutions. Sadly, religious life no longer seems capable of responding to this need, and therefore we detect the liminal witness surfacing in a whole range of alternative movements within and outside religious contexts. Many of the contemporary ecological and feminist movements serve the liminal calling in a truly authentic way. They name, bravely and subversively, the sins of oppression in this age and go beyond that to proffer alternative ways of living, for now and for the future. Liminality is alive and thriving, but for the greater part outside and not within the monastic and religious life we know today.

The present book does not offer a reform program for the vowed life. Instead, it seeks to surface the nature of the liminal challenge for our time. It seeks to highlight the struggle to live authentically and nonviolently in a world yearning for lasting peace and explores implications for how we live out the three traditional vows of poverty, chastity, and obedience. Through this approach, the reader is engaged in a discernment on how and where one is called to locate (or relocate) one's giftedness.

For contemporary religious the call of our time may be to place our resources (personal and congregational) more explicitly at the service of those movements that operate at the liminal cutting-edge in today's world. In many of our aging orders and congregations we ourselves may not feel able to assume the liminal work, but hopefully we can contribute to its unfolding through solidarity in prayer, thought, or supportive action.

In unraveling the meaning of each of the three vows and their significance for a world yearning for peace and harmony, I do not wish to dismiss or undermine the genuine faith and tremendous commitment that women and men of ages past brought to living the vowed life. Old paradigms had a certain relevance for their own time and, by and large, served us well in ages past. But they are often not relevant for our time. New needs require new responses; to use biblical language, new wine needs new wineskins (Mark 2:22). My intention is to retrieve deeper, archetypal meaning around those values that endure and sustain our effort to respond more fully to the God who calls us all to a more whole and authentic life.

CHAPTER TWO

The Nature of Vowed Commitment

No doubt the emphasis [on commitment] will be differ-
ent. It will fall less on chronological time and more on
existential totality. The important thing is not that one
spends a whole life doing something, but what one does
with one's whole life and how one does it.
— SANDRA M. SCHNEIDERS

A vow is a solemn promise underpinning a commitment to God or to another person. It is generally considered to be irrevocable, although in practice it is often revoked, as we experience in contemporary marriage. Whether within a religious or secular context, promising something under vow is considered to be as serious as swearing under oath. Giving of oneself in a total and genuine way is presumed to be at stake.

Solemnizing a vowed commitment in a public (ecclesiastical) context is a relatively recent and very much a Western development. In the great Eastern traditions, the vow was considered to be a private personal promise to God, taken and fulfilled with the support and supervision of the guru (or spiritual guide). In the Islamic tradition, even to this day, the vow denotes a serious commitment to fulfil specific duties of the Muslim faith, e.g., pray at the set daily times, go on pilgrimage to a sacred shrine (e.g., Mecca), give regularly to charity.

There are few prototypes in the Hebrew Scriptures for the Christian notion of vows. Rare references to the *nazir* signify an unconditional pledge of allegiance and submission to Yahweh — apparently more of a personal initiative rather than an institutionalized arrangement. And in the Christian tradition itself, it is only at the beginning of the thirteenth century that the three vows of poverty, celibacy, and obedience were confirmed with official legal status. The canonical implications of living the vowed life are very much a development of the nineteenth and twentieth centuries when Canon Law became an overriding factor in much of Christian theology and spirituality.

Our Fascination with Austerity

In seeking to explore the historical unfolding of the vowed life it is quite difficult to differentiate fact from fiction, lived practice from heroic asceticism. Our entire patriarchal culture — dating back some ten thousand years — tends to focus more on heroic deeds and achievements than on the vision that motivated such behavior. We focus on the externals, the observable data, but often bypass or totally ignore the internal motivation. In this way we often end up with a distorted and even thwarted vision of reality.

We also need to outgrow the religious sectarianism which underpins a great deal of what we consider the vowed life to be about. When depicting the great Eastern tradition of the monastic life, many writers sensationalize ascetical achievements, outstanding acts of endurance and sacrifice. Occasional comparisons with the West seem to serve no other purpose than to highlight the heroism of some above the others.

Our research and scholarship is particularly weak in the meager attention we give to prereligious forms of "vowed" commitment. I allude specifically to the long tradition of shamanism, which, as I outline elsewhere (O'Murchu 1991) merits close attention as a prototype for the monastic and religious life. In the shamanic experience we detect a very different quality of asceticism, a profound sense of cultural and earthly engagement aimed at grounding the devotee in a more coherent and spiritual relationship, not just with God, but with life in all its multifaceted dimensions. According to Abram (1996):

> The traditional or tribal shaman...acts as an intermediary between the human community and the larger ecological field, ensuring that there is an appropriate flow of nourishment, not just from the landscape to the human inhabitants, but from the human community back to the local earth. By his constant rituals, trances, ecstasies and "journeys," he ensures that the relation between human society and the larger society of beings is balanced and reciprocal, and that the village never takes more from the living land than it returns to it — not just materially, but with prayers, propitiations, and praise.... To some extent every adult in the community is engaged in this process of listening and attuning to the other presences that surround and influence daily life. But the shaman or sorcerer is the exemplary voyager in the intermediate realm between the human and the more-than-human worlds, the primary strategist and negotiator in any dealings with the Others.

It is this holistic tradition, grounded in everyday earthly experience, yet endowed with profound spiritual meaning, that I seek to reclaim in the present work.

Although verifiable evidence for ancient shamanism is meager — we rely a great deal on evidence from currently extant indigenous societies — we have developed sufficient mythological and anthropological skills to be able to make intelligent guesses at filling in gaps in our knowledge. When we use the technique and wisdom of a multidisciplinary approach we also stand a much better chance of achieving deeper spiritual insight and genuine discernment on the ancient foundations of our faith and spirituality. The strict scientific method, with its reliance only on what can be observed by the external senses, leaves us with a very impoverished, and frequently spiritually depraved, sense of reality.

De Dreuille (1975, 11ff.) introduces his analysis of Hindu monasticism with an observation on the caste system which prevailed in Hinduism almost from the beginning. The caste system creates a hierarchical ordering, giving all the power and privilege to those on the top; it is a blatantly patriarchal ploy. De Dreuille suggests that the evolution of Hindu monasticism is an attempt not so much to reform the caste system as to transcend it in seeking union with the God who is the principle of all order and transcends all human attempts at creating order in the world.

Hindu *tapas* (rigor of the austerities), therefore, should not be viewed in isolation, nor must we assume that they are ascetical practices similar to our Christian ascesis. The external behaviors serve a much deeper and more holistic purpose: the creation of a world governed by a more God-like sense of order. Not surprisingly, therefore, Hindu monastic spirituality focuses as much on the "three jewels" as on the three vows. The process of liberation (enlightenment) requires right vision, right knowledge, and right conduct. Four great virtues enhance this spiritual vision: universal friendship, seeing the good in all other creatures (inanimate included) and rejoicing in it, universal compassion, and tolerance of evil-doers (nonviolence).

We in the West are much more familiar with the Buddhist version of the monastic life, which in the East has developed in two main strands: the Theravada and the Mahayana. Foundational to all forms (and extremes) of Buddhist monasticism is precisely the same goal of the Buddhist belief system itself: the elimination of suffering by diminishing false desire. Once again the many rules and requirements are complemented (more accurately, preceded) by a set of basic virtues, described by de Dreuille (1975, 40) as "rightness of opinion (attitude), rightness of intention (thought), rightness of word, rightness of bodily activity, rightness of the means of existence, rightness of effort, rightness of attention, rightness of mental concentration."

Unfortunately, the burden of time and cultural conditioning has seriously undermined the value radiation which I believe is innate to the vowed life, in all its diverse cultural expressions.[5] Buddhist monks tend to take four vows, the first of which is to seek salvation for everyone. Universality underpins the vowed commitment. In the Mahayana tradition, the ideal to be aimed at in life is the attainment of buddhahood in a personal state known as the *bodhisattva*, a perfected state characterized by wisdom more than any other quality.

There is one outstanding difference between the *bodhisattva* status and the traditional notion of Christian perfection. The latter is generally understood as a complete separation from the world to facilitate a close personal relationship with God that will ensure personal salvation after death. The *bodhisattva*, on the other hand, vows not to enter the state of ultimate bliss (*nirvana*) until all creatures have been released from the cycle of rebirth and have attained perfection.

Contrary to the popular images associated with Eastern monasticism, in its fundamental essence it is much more person-centered and earth-based than our Western forms. While the mythic ascetical vision of the West focuses on escape into the barren desert where all desire and attachment are stripped away, the Eastern ideal is about return to the forest. The forest is a place of luscious growth, often wild and untamed. It is nature in its most natural, God-like state, devoid of the "refinements" imposed by human beings.

The forest, as symbol and metaphor, embodies some very ancient and deeply spiritual meanings. It is populated by trees, and for millennia before the emergence of formal religions, the tree was the primary symbol for the Great Earth Mother Goddess. The forest has a spontaneous natural wildness about it, a potential for the unexpected upsurge of the new, a dimension which Wilshire (1994, 52) associates particularly with the ancient understanding of the Virgin archetype; hence the phrase "virgin forest," denoting that quality of originality and an un-interfered-with state of nature where everything is in bud, bursting into flower and new life.

In Hindu spirituality, the third stage of development — aimed at inner journeying, along with the awakening and cultivation of enlightenment — is known as *banaprastha,* which literally means "dwelling in the forest." Whereas in the West, the inner journey is depicted as stripping away all physical, social, and mental attachment, the Eastern approach envisages a quality of engagement with life employing all the resources of person and planet alike. This salient strand in the monastic heritage of the East is rarely highlighted, bypassing, as in the West, what may well be the most ancient and enduring purpose of the vowed life.

Liminality and Perfection

In this chapter we are exploring the notion of commitment. In a culture of law, it is easy to envisage what this means; in a culture of value, there is not one clear-cut and absolute form of commitment. In a sense, the commitment has to be continually reworked as the enculturation of values requires. Where, therefore, is the continuity and stability? I suggest it is in the liminality which provides the grounding and context within which we live our commitment.

Commitment to a liminal way of life cannot possibly have the clarity and parameters of the more traditional image centered largely on the "way of perfection." Liminality is about growth and risk at the cutting edges. It requires fluidity and flexibility, creativity and courageous abandonment to divine recklessness. Metaphorically, it is encapsulated in the biblical image of the Jesus who "had nowhere to lay his head." The ideal monastic person of the West, often depicted as a heroic, ascetical Lone Ranger, forever battling with the forces of evil in the world, needs to be complemented with more incarnational images of both West and East.

The ideal holy person of the Eastern traditions — nearly always portrayed as male[6] — is not the one whose ultimate purpose is realized in a life of exclusive holiness here or in a state of perpetual happiness hereafter, but rather one who engages as fully as possible with the struggle in this life to attain that fulness of life to which God calls all people. In its original significance, the perfection entailed in the Eastern forms is not a completeness that can be attained, either here or hereafter, but rather an unfolding process that engages more deeply and more fully with the evolution of life itself.

This is not just a matter of two different cosmologies, a Western one that proffers the next world as the final goal of life after one earthly cycle and an Eastern approach based on the notion of reincarnation. We are dealing with something much deeper. And the depths into which we are plunging (or being plunged) are not, in fact, about the "next" life at all but about the present one, indeed about the eternal which we encounter at the heart of the created world itself.

In the great Eastern traditions the monastery and the *ashram* serve a very different purpose from the institutionalized models of our Western world. The traditional emphasis of the West, namely, that of escape, still haunts us, whereas the traditional emphasis of the East has been about engagement. The monastery is a type of energy-center that embodies and radiates the people's own deeper values. It serves as a type of cultural ideal for all that people hold dear in their hearts. Consequently, in many of the Eastern traditions (even to this day) it is the people and not the monks who recruit candidates for the monastery; the people will ensure that these centers of profound spiritual and cultural impact are always kept viable.

In short, the monastery is a nerve point of liminality. It provides a mirror image of what the people hold dear, but paradoxically a mirror that often reflects with a searing transparency and an intensity that often seems unbearable. Yes, the people themselves create the liminal spaces and will always ensure they flourish — within or outside formal religious contexts — but liminality always embodies more than either its creators or sustainers intend. It radiates the bittersweet, prophetic power of the cutting edge, calling us all to places we would rather not go.

As already outlined in chapter 1, liminality is first and foremost about value radiation, a locus for the intensification of those values which at depth we humans always cherish, although we may seek to express those values in confusing and contradictory ways. And the work of the liminal people is not about getting the values right, or living them out in perfect expression. The challenge is to engage with how we enculturate such values in the changing circumstances of time and culture — and, spiritually, we may add, enculturating the values in creative response to the new possibilities that God's Spirit is forever activating at the heart of creation.

Those called to vow themselves to this way of life face a daunting challenge. It is a vocation of depth and magnitude. Like the prophets of the Hebrew Scriptures it is a call that nobody gladly accepts, but one that requires a mysterious submission, made in the creative darkness of faith and trust. All the great traditions vouch for the divine nature of this call, and unfortunately all the traditions tend to spiritualize its essential meaning. Rarely, do we give due cognizance to (*a*) the role of human beings, who mediate the divine invitation and instigate the liminal movements, and (*b*) the mission of the liminal movement, which is about earthly and personal transformation in the unceasing renewal of God's creation.

The Language of the Vows

Traditionally, we use the preposition "of" to describe what the vows denote. We allude to the vow *of* poverty, *of* celibacy, *of* obedience. The use of the word "of" indicates that something is being contained, defined in terms of specific boundaries and characterized by clear-cut parameters. We think of a descriptive statement like "a glass of water." A certain quantity of water is contained within a specific object and thus becomes available to us in a functional and familiar way.

Applied to the vows, the preposition "of" strongly signifies function, one that has been legitimated legally over the centuries and now denotes clear-cut guidelines for living. The vows as presently and popularly understood set the boundaries for personal, communal, and moral behavior within which the person is expected to live and whose transgression incurs censures of various types, the ultimate one being expulsion from the order or congregation.

In this understanding, the legal connotation overrides all others. The vows are about laws that indicate what is and is not appropriate to the living out of the vowed life. And for a great deal of monastic history — East and West — people judged their success and commitment by the extent to which they followed the legal requirements of the vows. For much of that time, too, we lived with the unquestioned assumption that all religious law met with divine approval, indeed, more so, that the humanly instituted law automatically became God's law.

A reformulation of the vows is long overdue, and it seems to me that we cannot develop a new theology or spirituality of the vowed life without a radical change in the language we use. At the outset, I suggest we replace the preposition "of" with "for." It looks rather simple, but the shift in emphasis is quite substantial.

"For" is a much more generic word than "of." It denotes something to be done, to be achieved, a goal to be reached or a process to be activated. It denotes movement, action, growth, change, and possibility, but not necessarily an eventual outcome. It has echoes of freedom, creativity, initiative, possibility, exploration, search, and the expansion of horizons.

When we apply the preposition "for" to the traditional language of the vows, we immediately detect an incongruity. How can one speak of a vow "for poverty" in a world where poverty is such a scandalous evil; to opt "for celibacy" in today's world carries connotations of opting out of the spiritual challenge of our time to struggle to relate in a more loving and integrated way; to take a vow "for obedience" denotes subservience and passivity of a type that many people rightly consider to be suspect.

We are challenged to get behind the traditional language and surface the deeper meaning. This is an important hermeneutical task and not just a popular postmodern linguistic exercise. Over time our language does become denuded of real meaning; the original inspiration is often usurped and the ideological weight of time and tradition subverts the will-to-meaning that forms the basis of all ideas and words in the first place.

As we unmask the veil, the ideological veneer, and unload the religious baggage, we return to sources where the water tends to be purer. As Van Kaam (1968) hinted in the late 1960s, the vows expound fundamental values rather than fundamental laws. It is this rediscovery of the vows as archetypal values that guide our exploration and our renaming throughout the remainder of this book.

Commitment as a Spiritual Concept Today

Traditionally, one embarked upon a vowed commitment with the understanding that it would be life-long. In most religious cultures marriage denotes a similar total and life-long commitment. Commitment to the vowed life in the great Eastern faiths aims at the ideal of life-long allegiance, although in practice temporary expression is quite extensive and always has been. In the West, while temporary commitment has been considered, it has never been the subject of extensive experimentation, mainly, I suggest, because the permanent assent is considered to be the norm, and anything short of that smacks of compromise.

For Christianity, the theological foundation for life-long commitment tends to draw on the Hebrew notion of the covenant. Biblically, a commitment based on covenant takes as its starting point the God who forever remains faithful, whose fidelity is never withdrawn or compromised. In its true biblical sense, a covenant implies an invitation based on total commitment, because God's commitment to us is itself unconditional, unrelenting, and forever.

Covenant is not a certain type of religious commitment fashioned according to some set of human standards. Covenant is above all else an invitation based on a divine awakening. In one sense the one called is at the mercy of the one who calls, and yet, paradoxically, the response is made in freedom precisely because the overwhelming nature of the call is not one of greater confinement or limitation, but toward that fulness of life to which the gospels allude.

We tend to couch the notion of covenant in a quality of idealism that may be as inhibiting as it is inspiring. Undoubtedly, it does embody something of God's prodigious generosity, leaving some people with a perpetual sense of inadequacy and unworthiness, but for those who acknowledge that we are human and not divine, it enables an opening up to the transformation that God seeks to make possible in all our hearts. Does that transformation necessarily require life-long commitment — whether in marriage or in the vowed state of the religious life? The emphasis on life-long commitment envisaged in the covenantal relationship is itself initially construed in a distinctly patriarchal culture. The underlying ideals may convey more about the human will-to-power than about the divine desire for unflinching fidelity.

According to the American Jewish scholar Jon D. Levenson (1985), covenant in the Hebrew Scriptures has quite a precise connotation. It is closely interrelated with the concept of law, or Torah. It describes the relationship existing between two kings in which the more powerful would offer a relationship of suzerainty (a covenant) to the other, at the same time threatening that if a voluntary submission was not forthcoming, war would ensue.

The king of lesser status has a number of choices in how he can respond, but the choice of decline is never considered to be legitimate. Questions of obedience and disobedience are to the fore. The resulting ethos is one of uniformity and conformity. The exalted theological interpretation is used to validate the unquestioned monotheistic right of God, understood primarily (solely?) as a patriarchal overlord.

In what Elisabeth Schüssler Fiorenza calls the discipleship of equals, which she seeks to establish as the fundamental reality in the following of Christ, might we not need to seek out a different theology of covenant, one based not merely on a linear line of fidelity between the individual and God, but rather one of mutual coresponsibility exercised jointly (which is more suitable to the context of Christian marriage)? We also need to attend to the world of our day and its widespread and frequent waves of change. Commitment is always made in a cultural context. Fidelity to God at work in the world of our time may require fluidity and flexibility of a type largely unknown to previous generations. In the past people understood their sense of vocation as being in the one ministry and lifestyle for an entire lifetime; the chronological dimension seemed paramount. Nowadays, people change jobs regularly and frequently and often feel the call to move to something totally new as they seek to unravel and use their God-given talents; in the words of Schneiders, the existential dimension seems significantly more important at the present time:

> No doubt the emphasis will be different. It will fall less on chronological time and more on existential totality. The important thing is not that one spends a whole life doing something but what one does with one's whole life and how one does it. The important thing is not that one does not change one's state of life but that one does change, unceasingly, so as to be able to grow into

the fulness of life that was dimly outlined by the initial promise. It is this fundamental commitment to change and growth that allows us to see life commitment not as entrapment in static structures but as ongoing dynamic involvement with the whole of life, whatever the circumstances may be. (Schneiders 1986, 204).

The liminal vocation requires a large measure of fluidity and flexibility if it is to be lived creatively and in fidelity to the fundamental nature of that call. What is at stake is not a set of boundaries that need clear-cut parameters, cast in immutable legal structures, personal and institutional, but a set of horizons that require a creative and open-ended sense of engagement and ongoing exploration.

Commitment to New Horizons

The perceptual shift from boundaries to horizons is significant on a range of different fronts:

1. From the boundary of *formal religion* to the horizon of *human culture*. Religious life has become so institutionalized within formal religions that it is virtually inconceivable apart from them. By making religious life so religious we run the great risk of undermining its deeper meaning. We strip it of its radical originality as a people's movement, embedded in the human search for meaning in life and for those values that enable a more creative engagement with the surrounding culture. Only when we return the vowed life to its pristine role — as a global, cultural movement — will we learn to appreciate its deepest God-given significance.

2. From the boundary of *patriarchal control* to the horizon of *creative freedom*. Liminal witness of its very essence belongs to the cutting edge, the frontiers of new possibility. This space cannot be structured and controlled in accordance with the political and legal expectations of our Western (and Christian) norms. To do so runs the risk of destroying the

very uniqueness of the vowed life. And in the end, the greatest disservice will be to the very agents of that control, namely, human beings themselves.

3. From the boundary of *logic* to the horizon of *paradox*. Religious life in all cultures carries heavy connotations of legislating for every possible eventuality; this is a sure prescription to destroy the fundamental sense of mystery along with the promptings of the creative Spirit. Paradox is writ large in the tapestry of universal life, that apparently contradictory logic that leaves open the possibility of the new, the richness of diversity, and above all the possibility of being surprised by God. When law covers every conceivable outcome the chances are that it is law itself that has assumed the role of God, in which case those who implement the law are enmeshed in a web of idolatry.

4. From the boundary of *anthropocentrism* to the horizon of *divine freedom*. Like many aspects of contemporary culture (religion included), religious life has been crucified with reductionism and suffocated with minimalism. The masculine urge to manage and control so saturates the prevailing culture that it is difficult to confront, never mind change. We are scared in case things get out of control; we are frightened of innovation, creativity, and the power of the imagination. Yes, assuredly, we preach and proclaim the freedom of God's children — as long as it is contained within the church, approved by legitimate authority, and activated according to approved procedures. Little wonder that people often experience such freedom as yet another form of slavery.

5. From the boundary of *laws* to the horizon of *values*. Law carries with it very clear boundaries around what is possible and what is not, what is permissible and what is forbidden. Law has a great deal to do with feelings of being secure, of knowing where we stand, with people, with institutions, and with God. But is this security a feature of the Christian gospel? Or indeed of any of the major religions in their fundamental vision of hope and new possibility for humanity?

The call to the fulness of life, underpinning every God-given vocation, is inevitably one of searching, seeking, exploring, and risking. And the liminal call is above all else one of mutual engagement with those human yearnings and struggles to integrate values into our daily lives. This process of integration is not a once-and-for-all achievement, as the mainstream religions tend to assume, but a never-ceasing participation in the evolving and unfolding nature of universal life itself.

Evolution means, among other things, unceasing change, fresh calls to adaptation, and ever new invitations to engage with life's challenges and opportunities. There is no fixed blueprint, and there never has been. The immutability we humans attribute to God is more about *our* needs and projections than about God's essential nature.

While there do appear to be some foundational values to which all humans aspire — what elsewhere I describe as "archetypal" values (O'Murchu 1991) — attributing such values to some type of a fixed, unchanging divine nature helps neither to clarify the values nor to illuminate the meaning of divinity. Striving to live the values authentically and creatively will certainly awaken a sense of the numinous and the capacity to engage more deeply with mystery. In fact, the awakening sense of the divine will sometimes become more transparent in the messy struggle against injustice and suffering than in a lifestyle marked by harmonious and fulfilling relationships.

It is the enculturation of values that engages liminal witness, not their living-out in a coherent and distinctively Christian way, although that may be the goal we aim at. What authenticates the vowed life more than anything else is the willingness to risk everything in the process of value radiation. We encounter our ever-changing world in its light and in its darkness, and connect with those people and situations in seeking greater transparency for the fundamental gospel values of justice, love, peace, and liberation.

Keeping Vows or Living Them?

In the older understanding of vows, they are either observed, infringed, or mitigated. Observing, or keeping, the vow involves fidelity, first and foremost to God and second to those with whom we share such commitment. The relationship with God often becomes eschewed amid the plethora of laws and regulations that need to be fulfilled in living according to the requirements of one or another vow. The alienation from self and others that has often ensued from being faithful to the call to celibacy can scarcely be reconciled with the love and healing of the Christian gospel; nor can we assume that obedience to one's earthly superiors was always a guarantee of following the will of God; with hindsight, we can see that it clearly was not.

Breaking the law or infringing it is the inevitable dualistic opposite of keeping it. Today, we are rightly suspicious of all dualisms which create neat but superficial (and at times, highly dangerous) distinctions between what is acceptable and what is not. Increasingly, we realize that life is not as simple as most dualisms indicate; moreover, the real struggle which begets meaning and fresh hope arises not from adherence to one or another dimension of the dualism but from authentic commitment to the struggle that goes on in-between. According to an old Buddhist adage, perfection is not achieved in reaching the end of the road, but in walking the journey.

A real commitment to celibacy is not necessarily attained by never giving in to the desires of passion and intimacy, but by engaging with the daily struggle to live as more creative and loving human beings. As Moore (1992, 1994) and other contemporary writers highlight, it is this struggle that gives substance and soul to all our endeavors. Indeed, without such struggle we can never hope to encounter the power and potential of Christian incarnational living.

What the contemporary reader may fear more than anything else is the watering-down of idealism that many suspect to be at the root of everything I say about value radiation. Much of this fear may be grounded in a tendency to judge — oneself and others. While we hold on to the notion of the vows as laws, we find it easier to measure performance, our own and that of others. We assume that observing the vows keeps us in a right relationship with God, and infringing them distances us from God — all based on the highly questionable assumption that God thinks as we think, structures reality as we structure it, and judges as we judge.

Living the vows is quite a different invitation from keeping them. The former implies engagement with the issues of real life; the latter carries connotations of being at a distance from the world of reality, either away from it or superior to it. Keeping vows has strong moral connotations; living them has personal, interpersonal, and social implications. Keeping a vow still carries connotations of holiness and individual salvation, whereas living them requires a very different quality of spirituality, one which in fact is quite new even to the religions themselves.

Learning to Value in a New Way

Keeping vows carries with it a sense of holding on to something that never changes; it retains its unchanging significance from the day we commit ourselves to it. As we strive to live out our vows, we never cease to engage with change; how I live the vow of poverty in a wealthy Western European context requires a radically different response from that of being a slumdweller in São Paulo or Delhi. Context governs the criteria that make my liminal witness authentic or otherwise. Values are not static and unchanging; how I enculturate gospel values varies enormously from one part of the earth to another.

Sometimes it is easier to see the application of these principles to external rather than to internal situations. If we are to adopt nonviolence as an undergirding value for vowed living, we cannot escape the painful truth that much of our living in the past — our attempts to keep the vows — was itself fundamentally violent. Before we can move forward we must name, own, and hopefully outgrow our collusion with such violence.

I refer to issues that still remain important to many religious old and young in the various faith traditions of the world. I allude to the asceticism that frequently accompanied the observance of celibacy that often seriously violated the sacredness of the human body, the God-given giftedness of pleasure and eroticism, the capacity to relate in a warm and loving way. I allude to the privations endured in the name of poverty, often personally degrading and wasteful of time, energy, and money. Perhaps the most violent of all was the sheer oppression exerted in bending people's wills and evoking from them forms of submission that seriously undermined their dignity and freedom as incarnational human beings.

Moving out into the open arena of the world, some religious have colluded with the oppression of peoples in the two-thirds world "to win their souls for Christ." Whether we call it proselytizing or evangelizing, the respectability of the labels often masqueraded colonial and ideological brainwashing that can never be justified or exonerated. Despite our brave and original contributions to education and health care, we have often contributed to abusive practices, safeguarding the values of the governing systems rather than serving the people entrusted to our care. In the Christian context, our relationship with the formal church has frequently been collusive and potentially destructive. Rarely in recent decades have religious women stood openly for the rights and dignity of women, and those who did were often persecuted from within their own orders and congregations. Indeed, this internalized oppression has been quite widespread within religious life as it has been in the churches (and within the religions) generally.

There remains one strand of violence, fundamental to all

the others, that I seek to address in this book, that is, the betrayal of our liminal vocation, our failure to engage with the people's of our earth in their struggle to live in a more value-centered way. Central to that betrayal is our option to situate religious life within the context of formal church or religion. In this way, we cut ourselves off from the millions who do not follow any particular religion, and we also distance ourselves from millions even within the religions.

Religious life is not primarily about religion. It is a value radiation witness at the service of humanity. By restricting it to a religious context, we violate the very essence of our global and cultural outreach. We set limitations, restrictions, and even barriers to what we are meant to be about. Little wonder such betrayal has often come home to haunt us.

The call, therefore, to espouse a nonviolent vision is not just about a new way of being in ministry. It involves a massive shake-up of our entire way of life. It recalls us to priorities long subverted by the amnesia that belongs to patriarchal oppression. The task before us is to "re-member" our deep primordial story as a liminal movement at the service of humanity. We need to recall the ancient past, banished amid forced forgetfulness; we need to put back together the fragmented pieces, fractured so that religious dualisms could survive; we need to reconnect with the primal creativity of the human spirit which forever evokes liminal possibility at the cutting edge of new horizons.

We religious are like an estranged species, and at this moment a threatened one. We have lost our bearings. We have a great deal to reclaim, and there is an urgency about this retrieval. Hopefully, the present work will enable some among us, no matter how few, to make a fresh start. The radical option for nonviolent living is as good a starting point as any we can hope to embrace.

CHAPTER THREE

Celibacy: Is Nonviolent Sexuality Possible?

Sexuality's primary and perhaps supreme valency is the cosmological function.... Except in the modern world, sexuality has everywhere and always been a hierophany, and the sexual act an integral action and therefore also a means of knowledge. — MIRCEA ELIADE

For the ascetic position is one of the highest fear, the gravest immobility. The severe abstinence of the ascetic becomes the ruling obsession. And it is not one of self-discipline but of self-abnegation. — AUDRE LORDE

Celibacy is one of the oldest and most enduring of the three vows. In Christian religious life it entails a life-long commitment. This is also the ideal in the monastic systems of the other great religions, but the practice is somewhat different. Many Buddhist monks do in fact marry; the members of the Islamic Tariqahs tend to be married, but refrain from sexual relations when performing official duties within the orders.

In all the great monastic systems, celibacy denotes single-mindedness, an unencumbered devotion to God and to the development of the spiritual life. Implicit in this ideal is a cultural antagonism toward sexuality as something that is fundamentally alien to God and to spiritual growth. The assumption seems to be that spiritual growth and sexual fulfillment do not blend well together.

Consecrated celibacy in all the religious traditions is based on a spurious understanding of human sexuality, one I suggest that is fundamentally violent to both God and people. Sexuality is portrayed as belonging to the unruly passions and instincts which distract from the things of God. Sexuality is about pleasure and joy, which strangely we find unable to attribute to God and to God's creativity in the world.

And this leads us to deeper considerations. Sex in itself is not just the problem. There are several religious hang-ups around the human body and its God-given processes (see the classical and comprehensive work by Brown 1988). The body tends to be dualistically opposed to both the soul and the spirit. The body is deemed to be earthly, materialistic, prone to sin, an obstacle to the workings of divine grace. Consequently, the discipline and subjugation of the body plays a major role in early Christian asceticism and indeed in the monastic systems of all the great religions. Since sexuality is an integral dimension of our embodied existence the alienation of the body in the name of spiritual growth further convolutes the antisexual polemic that was already quite virulent.

Since the unfolding spiritual vision was very much the product of men and male thought patterns, it is not surprising that the female body and female sexuality became the primary and greatest casualty of this violent spirituality. Ironically, women, despite all their deficiencies, were deemed to be capable of strong sexual allurement, and their sexuality, more so than that of men, was deemed to be particularly unruly. The consequences are all too obvious even in the contemporary world. And the final aspect of this strange quagmire is the body of the earth itself; that, too, was to be shunned and spurned. Those called to the vowed celibate life were to flee the world, abandon it, and hate it as much as possible. The world, the flesh, and the devil all belonged to the one despicable package. Only a radical denial of all three, especially in the sexual realm, could guarantee entrance into life eternal.

Patriarchal Reductionism

Up until recent times we assumed that the antisexual polemic was inherent to religion generally and to Christianity
in particular. This is the way God ordained things (although
for centuries people have suspected that this was not the
case), and to question the package is to deny divine revelation itself. So we developed spiritual strategies to cope (and
allegedly grow in grace); we offered it up in sacrificial obedience to the will of God, and the more heroic we were in
discipline and asceticism the greater would be our reward in
the life to come.

For much of the Christian era, we were neither encouraged nor allowed to ask questions. Christian subservience
required total and unquestioned submission, until people began to realize that that was more about man's (literally) way
of doing things rather than God's. People at all levels of
religious adherence began to adopt "a hermeneutic of suspicion." We began to leave behind a religious infantilism and
grow up — often painfully — into the freedom and courage
that belong to the children of God.

A liberating option and, at times, a frightening one! Particularly frightening as one begins to realize that even God
himself/herself has also been subjected to patriarchal brainwashing. We begin to realize that formal religion may be
more of a human invention than a divine creation. We dis-
cover, thanks to several breakthroughs of modern science,
that God has been creatively at work in the world for billions
of years, yet religions construe the divine revelation as if it all
happened merely in the past few thousand years. The extent
to which formal religion has kept people in the darkness of
ignorance and superstition may well be the greatest violence
the world has known in the past five thousand years.

And as we unveil the ancient spiritual story of our human
and earthly evolution, we reconnect with powerful spiritual
movements that resonate deep in our primitive soul. We reconnect with the sacredness of our earth, with the female

face of God known to humans for over thirty thousand years during Paleolithic times, with the creative unfolding of God displayed in cycles and seasons of both the earthly and human body, and, finally, with sexuality, the primary source of ecstatic energy considered to be the core of God's own prodigious fertility.

Along comes religion, the final invention of the patriarchal will-to-power, and out goes all that had been happening for over thirty thousand years with the focus on the Great Earth Mother Goddess. That was the "paganism" that formal religion sought to eliminate. Little wonder that humanity today finds itself in the depths of alienation; little wonder that people in their thousands are flocking out of the mainstream religions.

The reader may wonder what all this has got to do with celibacy. Without this enlarged horizon of meaning, we cannot make sense either of what we are asked to transcend or what we are asked to assume as we try to reappropriate the liminal meaning of the vowed life. Context governs consciousness; how we perceive and conceptualize always belongs to a larger horizon of meaning. The old horizon was perceived to be unchanging and immobile. This often led to superficial spiritualization and a great deal of thwarted growth — spiritually and emotionally. But much more seriously, it created an ideology of religious belief that sought to destroy some of the most sacred aspects of our sacred story as an evolutionary species.

Let me illustrate my concern in direct relation to the vow of celibacy. A great deal of the spiritual undergirding for Christian celibacy over the centuries has been the modeling offered in the name of the Blessed Virgin Mary. According to Christian teaching, Mary was deemed to have conceived Jesus without sexual intercourse and gave birth without losing her physical virginity. Virginity in its basic biological meaning was exalted to the status of a divine quality, solemnized in 1854 when the Catholic Church declared Mary's Immaculate Conception to be an article of faith.

As we scan through the recurring myths of prereligious times, a number of archetypal themes frequently occur. These are constellations of key values relating to the meaning of daily life and often are depicted as assuming personal significance. We find several myths around the Hero, the Warrior, the Lover, the Great Mother, the Crone, and the Virgin. But "virgin" in this ancient context has a very different meaning from that fostered in the mainstream religions:

> For early cultures, the word "virgin" did not mean "one who has never had sex." In its primal sense the word "virgin" describes a maiden, a very young woman who is leaving girlhood, just beginning to explore and taste her grown-up Self. She is in bud — full of potential, unfinished, entering the unknown in a state of joyous uncertainty. Such a one is full of wonder and becoming, curious about all the possibilities in herself and the world — open to the mysteries and dangers that lie ahead. Clarity does not apply to her, for She is in process, in-between. Anticipation, freedom, and spontaneity do describe her. She is highly susceptible to falling in love — with the dawn, with the changing seasons, with any and all creatures in their miraculous diversity, with people, their eyes and stories. For whatever the risks, the virgin experiences Nature as full of good things, and gifts, full of possibility. (Wilshire 1994, 49).

As the mainstream religions unfold we witness a gradual reductionism of the original archetype from something creatively ennobling to a stilted, unfertile biological state. Even in the Hebrew Scriptures, we see some attempt to retain the original meaning when the writer of Isaiah 7:14 uses the word *parthenos,* which archetypally signifies a heightened state of fertility wherein one can conceive without the assistance of male impregnation. Although the Christian gospels quote the text from Isaiah they continue the insidious process of reductionism. This sinister subversion of feminine creativity is even more degrading in Islamic culture: the woman whether single or married is made as invisible as possible, right down to how she dresses in public places.

The cult of virginity is a powerful patriarchal ploy, not merely to subdue women in contemporary culture, but to subvert the long historical tradition of women's special access to divinity and its prodigious potency for sexual becoming. The one religion that retains something of this ancient wisdom is Hinduism, where many of the great godly figures (male and female) are depicted in voluptuous and highly sensuous embrace. Sexual ecstasy is at the core of divine creativity.

Undoing the Violent Subversion

The inherited tradition underpinning the vow of celibacy rests on a number of quite violent assumptions, violent in the sense that they deviate from the very purpose which God seems to have designed for sexuality and its uses in human and planetary life.

First, all humans are sexual beings. Our sexuality is essential to our self-identity. It is our sexuality that activates that capacity to relate whereby we come to know the self and the other and the interactive mutuality that is the central experience of what it means to be human. More than any other aspect of our selfhood, our sexuality establishes our human uniqueness.

Yet, for centuries, religion has tried to sidetrack this core element of our selves. Over many centuries, formation in the religious life has encouraged millions to become asexual, allegedly like the angels in heaven. Even in marriage, sex was held to be suspect. The antisexual polemic, perpetuated by formal religion, has a particularly obnoxious feel to it and has the potential to be enormously destructive.

Second, religion assumes that God wants to have little or nothing to do with sexuality. God is also portrayed as being asexual. Sex more than anything else alienates the person from God. The monotheistic religions are particularly vicious in their antisexual bias that is nearly always accompanied by the popular perception that God, in his real essence, is also a disembodied being. Even Christians have been swept along by this heresy.

Religion's desire to desexualize God probably dates back to the rise of patriarchy itself (around 8000 B.C.E.) when the prevailing spirituality (which the patriarchs call "paganism") exhibited a strong sexual orientation. The prodigious creativity of the Great Mother Goddess, that wild and often uncontrolled exuberance, was quite overtly sexual, and the many sexual hang-ups that prevail today seem to have been largely unknown at that time. But the playfulness of this ancient culture militated against the growing masculine urge to "conquer and control," and, sadly, sexuality became the primary victim of a repressive regime that was to last for subsequent millennia.

Third, sexuality represents that aspect of personality that has to do with feeling and emotion, with passion and playfulness. The culture of formal religion, especially in the monotheistic traditions, shuns the expression of heart and exalts the rationalism of the head. By favoring the process of deductive reasoning, the power of imagination could be subverted.

Not surprising, therefore, we note that ritual and worship, which for millennia used dance, music, and trance-like behavior to relate with the divine-human mystery, in the formal religions becomes structured, institutionalized, and progressively devoid of feeling, emotion, and real human meaning. Little wonder that people abandon the staid and empty ritualism of contemporary religion.

Because humans have been encouraged to split off the feeling and emotional dimensions of themselves, we find in today's world a series of highly destructive projections of sexualized energy. Our sexuality is a form of psychic energy, always seeking expression. If we refuse to channel it in creative ways, we inevitably end up projecting the bottled-up energy onto scapegoats, and this is the basis for so much irresponsible sexual acting-out at the present time.

Innocent and vulnerable people are often the victims of our sexual projections. But the cumulative effects are even more frightening. The repressed sexual energy of our collective culture is projected, more than anywhere else, into the weapons of warfare and mass destruction, many of which have an unmistakable phallic identity. Hence we hear in every modern war of mass rape of innocent women, often carried out by soldiers on their own citizens. And it is not by chance or accident that SCUD missiles (with their distinctive phallic appearance), although aimed at cities on mountaintops, frequently end up in vulva-type valleys.

Finally, the religious culture blindly colludes with the contemporary mechanization of sex. This is very much a development of the sixteenth and seventeenth centuries that emphasizes sex as function, sex for the purpose of procreation. This is the final layer of the cake of sexual repression, a last-ditch effort to strip it as completely as possible of any sense of joy, creativity, and sacredness. Ironically, the religions get sucked into yet another collusion with the prevailing culture and seek to sanction the aberration by attributing the procreative power as much as possible to the distant, asexual God.

The final decades of the twentieth century were marked by a subtle but worldwide reaction to the mechanization of sex. People decided that they were going to reclaim the joy and pleasure of sex, and they did not even consider how the dominant institutions of church or state might respond. In fact, some institutions like the Catholic Church responded positively, changing its theology of marriage in 1962.[7] But the floodgates had been opened and the repression of centuries began to pour out — creating an enormous sense of liberation and searing levels of abuse and exploitation.

The major shift of the past few decades has not been publicly acknowledged. The major institutions, and the culture at large, are in such deep denial that they have not been able to read the signs, an upheaval that will probably change permanently the very meaning of human sexuality. I allude to the widespread practice of giving genital sexual expression to many forms of human intimacy, whether between male and female or between people of the same sex. Sexuality has broken out, not merely of the exclusive realm of monogamous marriage, but also out of the traditional context of heterosexual partnerships. Perhaps, most important of all, the deep collective desire of humanity seems to be that it should also transcend the specific focus on procreation of the species.

Ironically, we seem closer now than ever before to that understanding of human sexuality that prevailed in pre-patriarchal times. Whereas the dominant culture today is often perceived as one that is swamped in sexual hedonism, promiscuity, and permissiveness, a much deeper transformation is also at work. Like all classical paradigm shifts the mixture of light and shadow is all too apparent.

The guardians of orthodoxy are quick to highlight the darkness and its potential for destruction, but potentially much more destructive is the violence we do when we fail to perceive and discern the deeper messages. As I suggested in previous chapters, this is uniquely the work of liminal movements, and for the remainder of this chapter I want to focus on the liminal challenge of renaming the sexual revolution that is erupting around us and uncovering the deeper cultural and spiritual significance of this transformation.

Sexuality in Its Liminal Context

Lest the reader be confused, let me assert quite unambiguously: yes, I am suggesting that the liminal engagement with the major sexual questions of our time is the primary responsibility of those called to consecrated celibacy. The integrity and authenticity of the call to celibacy is not dependent upon the ascetical ability to forego sexual engagement, but upon a quality of engagement — emotionally and spiritually — that touches the very depths of sexual aestheticism. Hence my proposal that we leave behind a spirituality focused on law and adopt one focused on value. We also need to abandon the traditional language "of celibacy" and adopt the phrase "for relatedness"[8] which I will use for the remainder of this chapter.

The *vow for relatedness* is a call to engage with the emerging issues of psychosexual relating in the contemporary world, to read the unfolding reality with discernment and sensitivity, to unearth the deeper, archetypal meanings of this unfolding, to name the unfolding process in a way that is holistic and liberating, to highlight the spiritual implications of this new understanding, and to promote social and political strategies to reintegrate what for so long we have split off in our destructive asexual, disembodied ways of living.

The liminal vocation is, of its very nature, highly paradoxical; this is what safeguards its essential mysterious and divine nature. In traditional biblical terms the liminar is in the world, but not of it. The liminar is a full sexual person, with all the feelings, emotions, desires, and possibilities of that deeply creative urge. But the call to the liminal space requires a different way of living out our sexual relatedness.

Traditionally, this has been interpreted as refraining from all types of sexual and genital interaction in a single lifestyle, with community living offered as the antidote to meet emotional and relational needs, but in a nonsexual way.

As already indicated, this interpretation carries an inherent violence against self and others. It is a fundamental denial of our God-given identity to choose a nonsexual way of life; it is an act of blasphemy. Biologically, psychologically, and spiritually, we cannot become asexual. The more we try, the more our sexual selves will rear up in protest.

Our sexuality consists of all those feelings, moods, and emotions that require a certain quality and quantity of human closeness, intimacy, tactility, and love if we are to become, and help each other become, the fully evolved people that God intends us to be. To choose to forego this call is an act of violence against God, self, and those other people who befriend us on the journey of life.

In recent years, many in the vowed life have come to acknowledge the destructive implications of pretending not to be sexual in one's essential nature. Attempts to reappropriate a more integrated way of being sexual while still being celibate have not been easy. One-sexed communities, in the case of male groups particularly, do not seem to be the most appropriate context for warm and supportive mutuality. In practice, people tend to have their emotional needs met outside, rather than within, one-sexed communities.

There is a great deal of confusion on how best to integrate the genital dimension of our sexuality. Many who advocate a more intimate and open way of celibate relating strongly exclude any form of genital expression; to move in that direction would be considered by many to be an even more destructive and violent thing to do. This is a delicate subject that requires a great deal of reflection, dialogue, and discernment.

In the long tradition of the monastic and vowed life, the requirement not to be married automatically meant total abstinence from all forms of genital and physical intimacy. In the culture generally, genital sexuality was perceived as belonging only to the realm of marriage. Officially, all the religions still endorse this arrangement, although in the culture generally those two realities are no longer connected. Genitality has become a dimension of intimacy in many non-marital situations. This development is often attributed to contemporary liberal attitudes and behaviors. It is a great deal more complex than this. In fact, as a species we may be experiencing an evolutionary shift in our understanding of human sexuality that is impacting significantly upon all of us, single, married, and celibate alike. (For further elucidation, see Evola 1983; Nelson and Longfellow 1994; Eisler 1995).

In terms of its countercultural witness, it makes a great deal of spiritual sense that the vow for relatedness should require nonmarital status; it also sets the liminar free to engage more fully with the global, cultural landscape of liminal witness. Whether or not the celibate should totally refrain from sexual, genital intimacy, in a world where such intimate expression is no longer tied exclusively to marriage, it has at least to remain an open question.

Even if the celibate refrains from genital intimacy, the liminal person must be able to share something of the deep internal growth and struggle that characterizes sexual unfolding in human life. This is a divinely ordained process that we dismiss to the mutual destruction of self and others. And to engage meaningfully with this process, the celibate needs to be a warm, tender, and sensitive person, not cold, clinical, and disembodied in one's essential nature. One cannot be passionate about one's liminal calling without being in touch with the fires of passion that burn within. As celibate people, it is our sexuality more than anything else that fires us for that dangerous and daring witness that makes our liminality credible.

Set My People Free

The liminal space has no hidden agendas, no toxic secrecy, and no labels that violate reality into falsity. It is the space where, on behalf of God's people, the liminars are called to speak the unspeakable, say the unsayable, and offer new texts for the weary rhetoric of our oppressive past.

Those called to live the vow for relatedness at the liminal cutting edges face the daunting task of ridding our world of thousands of years of sexual repression. The opposition will be momentous, particularly from the patriarchal forces that require the repression to keep people under control; and when that is embroiled in religious dogmatism, it becomes even more difficult to shift and change perspective.

There is a great urgency to reclaim the fundamental good-
ness, joy, and pleasure of sex. We need to retrieve the long
subverted tradition, the one our species knew for thousands
of years before the age of patriarchy, in which sexuality was
perceived as the primary quality of the divine, a passionate creative energy, deeply imbued with spiritual potency. In
the collective unconscious of our species there lies a secret
suspicion that sex is the way to God and the way to holiness. We need to come home to ourselves as spiritual, sexual
people and once more inhabit the land of our collective inner
wisdom.

To do this we need to demolish many of the categoriza-
tions that were created to promote the philosophy of "divide
and conquer." We label sexual orientation as heterosexual,
homosexual, or bisexual, and we invest a great deal of time
and energy trying to convince ourselves that life is construed
according to our man-made categories. As sexual creatures
our sexuality is a unity that can assume various expressions
throughout the course of a lifetime. Above all else, it is not a
mechanistic device to procure and guarantee the propagation
of the species.

To outgrow the mechanization of sex and reclaim its essentially spiritual and humanizing affect is the only way to
demolish both the repression and oppression that dominate
the world today. The gross pornographic acting-out, on the
one hand, and the secret inner guilt-ridden turmoil, on the
other, are each the product of the same repressive regime,
and one is as violent and destructive as the other. In fact, it
is the inner repression that often fuels the projections that
feed the sexual pornography of today's marketplace.

To outgrow the violence, we need to reclaim a wholesome
sense of freedom, the gospel freedom that is about justice and
true love, what the theologian Rebecca Chopp (1989, 107–
15) calls "emancipatory transformation." We need to learn
afresh how to befriend our sexuality with its light and darkness, pleasure and pain, instincts and intuitions. We need to
be able to enjoy the embodied feelings of pleasure and good-

ness that belong to our sexualized selves. And we need to be able to relate with significant others with a quality of tenderness, closeness, and affection that begets deeper love and meaning in life-giving mutuality.

And since our sexuality is a powerful erotic force, which can plunge us to the depths of passion or of pain, we need to hold this energy with the protective layer of care and discipline. We know only too well the destructive aftermath of dissipated sexual acting-out, the broken trust, the hurt feelings, the deeper inner alienation, the emotional scars that can continue to fester over an entire lifetime. But the discipline for our time is not necessarily the heroic, internal asceticism of bygone days, but a mutual discipline, requiring honest and appropriate disclosure, sincere engagement in the process of sexual integration, and prayerful appreciation for this creative but volatile gift with which all humans are blessed.

The freedom I write about is very different from the so-called sexual liberalism which characterizes the public forum of today's world. What dominates the sexual landscape today is not liberalism but confusion — about the meaning of sex, the nature of sex, and the divine-human identity which cannot be fully understood without a wholistic view of human sexuality. In large part, the confusion is the product of our inherited past, but its prevalence in the present time might equally well be the result of a culture ravished because of liminal deprivation. Without that unique quality of light that befits liminal witness, the forces of darkness become all the more pervasive.

At the present time there is no creative forum in which we can encounter our true selves as psychosexual people. There is no prophetic space where the real issues can be talked about, prayed about, and lived out anew. What we encounter in today's world is a cutting edge of painful projections, and like all projection, heavily camouflaged in denial; that is the shadow material, which also needs to be befriended in whole new ways. But where is the complementary light? Buried, I suggest, beneath layers of dysfunctional liminality, because

the liminars of our time (officially those who follow the monastic and religious way of life) have lost touch with the fire
that burns within.

To set the people free, the liminars themselves must be
liberated. As I have explored elsewhere (O'Murchu 1991,
1995), this is likely to require a paradigm shift of death-
resurrection proportions for the vowed life. Meanwhile, we
need to be attuned to the seedlings of new life that the creative Spirit begets amid the aridity and barrenness of this
time of waiting. From the liminal point of view, we don't
have to wait for a new wave of religious life to be born. It is
the people themselves who engender liminal possibilities, and
the people will always ensure that liminal energy is at work
at the cutting edges of human life and culture.

Precisely, for this reason, we cannot dismiss the sexual
horizons of our time as merely the product of permissiveness and promiscuity. There *is* a deeper meaning (eruditely
illustrated by Moore 1998), and already many people are in
touch with the deeper message. Many people in counseling
and therapy know what's going on; so do the many people
who engage in wholistic spiritual direction. And in a paradoxical way, those we label as promiscuous are often in tune
with the deeper questions we are exploring. Here it may be
worth recalling that Jesus commended prostitutes as among
the first who gained access to the New Reign of God. Jesus
recognized the deeper story; unfortunately, we rarely do.

Who Cares for the Sexual Liminars?

Of all the issues confronting those called to the vowed life,
the vow for relatedness makes the heaviest demands. The
risk of being overwhelmed is ever close at hand. Traditionally, religious were admonished to protect their celibate
integrity by lives marked by prayer and discipline; the onus
rested very much with the individual person. More recently,
the emphasis has shifted to the need for good quality com-

munity life where basic needs for befriending, dialogue, and mutuality can be met in a nonsexual way.

The desired communal outcome is undermined by two dominant factors: (*a*) the personal baggage from the past which still considers sex to be too sensitive a subject for responsible human dialogue; and (*b*) the cultural, especially religious taboo, that tends to drive sexual energy underground into toxic secrecy or outward in destructive projections, thus never allowing humans to come home to themselves as fundamentally sexual people. As already indicated, the communal undergirding is experienced by many contemporary religious outside rather than within their formal communities.

The journey to sexual wholeness today, the call to nonviolent intimacy, requires not one but several types of support, challenge, and affirmation; and these are as relevant for the married person as for the celibate or those opting for a single way of life. The following elements will require ongoing attention, dialogue, and discernment:

- our psychosexual identity (the who of our existence)
- awareness of what's going on (the why)
- friendship and mutuality (the how)
- embodiment (the how)
- sexuality and justice
- prayerful contemplation for liminal solitude
  (see Nouwen 1986, esp., 21–48).

1. *Identity.* Personally and collectively we must outgrow the violent denial of the past, the pretense that we could live like some type of divine angelic creatures, devoid of all sexual thought or feeling. Our sexuality is at the very core of what it means to be human, innate to the *imago dei* in which we are all created.

We must learn afresh to befriend this divine gift, with its volatile mixture of light and shadow. We must create a language whereby we can communicate, dialogue, and relate in a more coherent and constructive way as sexual people. Aided by God's grace and supported in a more transparent human way, we can then begin to come home to our true selves as sexual people.

The call to outgrow the repression and suppression of the past and replace it with a more wholesome and integrated understanding of human sexuality is a challenge for celibate and noncelibate people alike. For the celibate, it is a primary responsibility of liminal witness, an undertaking that requires, from the outset, dialogue and engagement with other people, married and single. We are dealing not with an issue related to some exclusive type of holiness (as in bygone days) but about an incarnational gift that engages every human person on the journey to wholeness.

2. *Awareness.* Our sexuality is not a static, mechanistic, biological function, given once and for all, and never possible of change or modification. It is first and foremost a divine, erotic energy, an intense psychic presence, activated in every human yearning for intimate and creative expression.

We carry an appalling ignorance about the meaning of our sexuality, clouded not just by centuries but by millennia of patriarchal violation. Sex and gender modeling has been subverted into the forces of hostility and the attainment of power. Long before the permissiveness of the 1960s and thereafter, sexual violence had a long and triumphant reign. Ironically, it has taken something as perverse as the promiscuity of the 1960s to initiate the process of sexual liberation.

The current modeling — of sex for procreation, within a monogamous heterosexual relationship, protected by the permanent bond of marriage — is crumbling all around us. As a model it has positive qualities, perhaps ones that have endured the test of time. And its demise cannot be attributed to the promiscuity and permissiveness of this age. Something much deeper and more complex is at work, and we need to mobilize our resources of awareness, wisdom, and discernment to decipher the deeper message.

This is where the liminars must step forward and begin to retell a new sexual story for our time. Not entirely new, because, as indicated previously, some very ancient sexual motifs — especially creativity and spirituality — are once again being evoked. The rediscovery of sexual power and passion is a process where liminal people are called to take many initiatives. Our failure to do so is not merely a failure of nerve but a betrayal of the divine call to be God's cutting-edge agents on behalf of the human family.

3. *Friendship and Mutuality.* In the darkened condition of our hearts and minds today — the violent aftereffects of the age of repression — allusions to sex and sexuality tend to conjure up notions of genital activity. Genital tyranny still reigns over our hearts and imaginations.

As indicated previously, the genital aspect is only one — albeit an important — dimension of our sexual reality as a human species. Much more basic is the need to experience and negotiate love, intimacy, tenderness, and mutuality. These are features of human life that none of us can do without; deprived of these qualities we stand little chance of realizing our full potential as incarnational human beings.

Traditionally, celibate living assumed quite a degree of isolated individuality. Celibacy was perceived to require a special relationship between the devotee and God, making human friendship largely unnecessary. This often produced a sour celibacy, devoid of warmth and the capacity to express affection or tenderness — needs often met in the celibates themselves through charitable work or apostolic action.

The vow for relatedness requires above all else a well-developed capacity to relate warmly and lovingly with other human beings. Human friendships are important, some of which will be special and require deeper levels of reciprocity (see the informative study of Hunt 1982). The balance between meeting needs for love within and outside community requires a quality of transparent dialogue that is still a rare commodity.

Whatever the tensions, challenges, and risks, the choice to

have close human friendships and to devote time and energy
to their development is nonnegotiable for celibate living of
the future. It is the struggle to engage deeply in our own
emotional and erotic unfolding that authenticates our liminal
transparency as we seek to engage with the complex dynamics that living lovingly and tenderly requires in the world of
our time.

4. *Embodiment.* Contemporary feminist literature docu-
ments in great detail the horrific debasement of the body —
especially the female body — that has taken place under
the aegis of patriarchy (e.g., Graham 1995, Heyward 1989,
Raphael 1996). The sexual repression, often referred to in
this chapter, is felt more painfully in the body than in any
other sphere of our personalities. It has left some people in
deep emotional and physical pain, others with very negative
self-images, and others forever trying to compensate in the
contemporary cult of the "body beautiful."

Paradoxically, the forces of repression accurately state
that sexuality is an embodied energy, in fact the very force
that brings flair, passion, intensity, and elegance into all our
living. In saying this, however, let us remember that the
embodiment of our sexuality is as much a collective as an individual phenomenon. In fact, all our embodied sexual needs
are experienced in their richer and fuller meaning in mutual
engagement with others.

We have also tended to equate genitality with the embodied aspect of sexuality, and this has seriously depleted
our appreciation of ourselves as embodied as well as sexual
people. In fact, the psychic energy that awakens sexual desire and instinct belongs more to the mind (and spirit) than
to the body in its material sense.

As a sexual concept, embodiment takes on a whole new
meaning today, stretching our incarnational intuitions toward new and largely unexamined possibilities. These are
the new awakenings that liminal people need to nurture and
cultivate. We experience a growing sense of the universe itself as body, requiring us to revisit the ancient wisdom that

perceived Planet Earth as the body of the Great Mother Goddess.

Retrieval of this long subverted spiritual ferment is becoming a central concern in contemporary theological reflection (e.g., McFague 1993, Edwards 1995). Theology and ecology are forging a new alliance as each grapples with the ethical and ecological concerns for the future of the earth-body itself. The passion driving this new consciousness is itself a core value of our human sexuality.

5. *Sexuality and Justice.* The feminist theologian Carter Heyward (1988) claims that the passion of sexuality is what also awakens in us a passion for justice and right relationships across the entire spectrum of life and meaning. According to Brock (1992, 40), "The erotic compels us to be hungry for justice at our very depths because we are response-able. We are able to reject what makes us numb to the suffering and self-hate of others."

As distinct from the *apatheia* (passionlessness) advocated from earliest Christian times, today we experience the call of the gospel as a call to life, to the wholeness that is released by living interdependently in our world. The passion within and the passion without synchronize in whole new ways. In the words of the black feminist poet and essayist Audre Lorde (see Plaskow and Christ 1989, 213), "Recognizing the power of the erotic within our lives can give us the energy to pursue genuine change within our world, rather than merely settling for a shift of characters in the same weary drama."

While pride and passion were one time construed as the road to perdition — more accurately key feminine values that the patriarchal culture could not tolerate — today apathy and indifference are the cancerous parasites of our age, and as John O'Donohue (1997, 91) astutely remarks

> indifference is necessary for power; to hold control one has to be successfully indifferent to the needs and vulnerabilities of those under control. Thus, indifference calls for a great commitment to non-vision....

> When you become indifferent, you give all your power
> away. Your imagination becomes fixated in the limbo of
> cynicism and despair.

Meanwhile our passionate energy is either numbed or dissipated amid the plethora of lurid and empty promises. The
engagement with pleasure and pain is often reduced to the
"satisfaction" of a quick fix, a fleeting sensation that pro-
cures neither intimacy nor justice. The way out is not more
control over our sex drive, but a radical reappropriation of
who we really are as people gifted with passionate and erotic
creativity.

6. *Solitude and Prayer.* Over the centuries the vocation
to celibacy was virtually suffocated with spiritualism. All
the passionate and erotic feeling had to be subdued or
sublimated, because it was construed as contrary to God's
apatheia and consequently was an obstacle to progress in
the spiritual life. The violence engendered is all too obvious to require further comment. The healing required in the
aftermath is now a major issue for our times.

The need to situate the celibate vocation in a contemplative context of prayer and solitude is as necessary for married
and single persons as it is for celibates. It is not so much our
sexuality that requires a special quality of spiritual address as
our liminality. It is the precarious marginalization of our calling that requires us to engage with psychosexual questions
from a deeply reflective and discerning space.

The contemplative stance required is one centered in the
world of daily reality and not from within some secluded
monastery or hermitage — although that, too, may be an
important dimension of the liminal spiritual journey. The
contemplation I write about is a solitude of the heart that
strives to be deeply present to the call of our world and to
the stirrings of the creative Spirit. Above all else it is about
perception, about seeing, and seeing in depth.

Drawing on the contemplative vision of Thomas Merton,
Joan Chittister (1990, 52, 57) describes contemplation as

"the ability to see through, and to see into, and to see despite and to see without blindness.... It is the ability to see a whole world rather than a partial one." It is the wisdom of the heart that enables us to see the illusions that masquerade as reality, the constructs that time has hallowed but are really the hollow constructs of the human will-to-power. It is also the wisdom that digs deeply, seeking to unearth and reclaim what has been lost and subverted, so that once more we can retrieve the *whole* story of who we are in our essential God-given nature.

It is from this depth that we begin to reclaim our real story as a psychosexual species, endowed with the erotic propensity to relate in love and justice, not merely with other humans, but with all those creatures who populate our world, and with the earth itself as the cosmic womb of erotic possibility.

The Great Retrieval

I end this chapter by returning to the opening quote in which Audre Lorde refers to traditional sexual asceticism as a "ruling obsession." The nature of this obsession has been depicted in graphic detail in a range of contemporary feminist writings (Daly 1973, 1978; Morgan 1989). Throughout the entire Christian era and indeed for long before it, human sexuality was the target of attack and subjugation. It was the erogenous driving force that seems to have posed an enormous problem for our patriarchal forebears. Consequently, it became probably the single greatest victim of the masculine compulsion to divide and conquer.

In concluding this chapter I allude briefly to the gender issue, which is also central to our considerations. The patriarchal fear of sexuality was fundamentally a fear of the power of the feminine which men seem to have perceived as being exclusive to women. In the wake of the Agricultural Revolution, female creativity began to pose a huge threat to the emerging male prominence and the masculine urge to be in charge of the world and its evolution. To do that the goddess had to be conquered and subdued, and the most effective way to do it was eliminate (as far as possible) those fostering and promoting her vision.

In these ancient cultures, the emerging evidence seems to suggest that women played a predominant role as culture-makers. This suggestion leads many scholars into the exploration of a matriarchal culture in which women exercised power and control; this is yet another projection from the present into the past, and seems an unhelpful line of inquiry.

Where the women seem to have dominated was in their engagement with fertility and pleasure; they led the way in a highly sexualized society, where sex itself was considered to be a primary quality of the Great Goddess. This gave women unique access to a potential for creativity and imagination. It encouraged a culture of connection and relatedness, an egalitarian climate verging on a sacred utopia. Violence was largely unknown in this ancient culture; even hunting practices were highly ritualized. The female consciousness wanted to befriend the earth and its potential for creative becoming; the men wanted to conquer it and become the creators themselves. This is where the clash began, and this, I submit, is what triggered the rise of patriarchy (more on this topic in Eisler 1995).

A celibacy for nonviolence needs to retrieve these very ancient roots to make sense to its devotees, but, much more importantly, to make sense to the surrounding culture. The liminal implications of the vow for relatedness are quite complex (and we do it violence by simplifying it in canonical or spiritualized terms), yet profoundly connected to the search for sexual meaning in this age as in every other.

The violence we are invited to confront and transform is not merely the promiscuity and pornography which lead to such gross exploitation in our world today. This is merely the surface expression of a cultural repression that has very deep roots. As a human species we are often torn between a repression of toxic secrecy and a massive cultural projection that overwhelms us sensually and emotionally. Between these two extremes is the precarious and vulnerable pilgrimage of coming home to ourselves as psychosexual beings. Laying the paving stones for that pilgrim path is the onerous and privileged responsibility of liminal people.

A great deal of the liminal work is about "permission giving." It is okay to be a sexual person and to feel the full repertoire of sexual feeling and emotion. And it is okay to talk about it and to seek out a vocabulary whereby we can connect and relate. It is also okay to give expression to one's vulnerability and woundedness, and practically everyone of us carries wounds within our sexual selves.

And there is another quality of "permission giving" that both invites and requires us to engage with the profound sexual questions of our time. It is okay to seek out those skills — spiritual, social, political, and, above all, prophetic — we need to engage with the momentous and complex realities we encounter.

In being called apart to the liminal spaces, we do not withdraw from the world. Rather we engage in a whole new way with the perennial questions of meaning and hope that awaken possibilities for Christian resurrection in each new epoch of human evolution. To be discerning people at that exciting horizon, we need to equip ourselves with all the human and spiritual resources we can mobilize. And let us never forget that the wise and loving God who calls us to the liminal places will provide us with more than enough resources for the task ahead. With that reassurance in our hearts, we can befriend all who seek to outgrow the violence of the past and engage for the future in those creative and constructive relationships that will beget a more just and harmonious world for all humankind.

CHAPTER FOUR

The Violence of Consumerism and Deprivation

*The final hope of Christians is not heaven, but partici-
pation in God's restoration of all things.*
— GORDON ZERBE

*A healed relation to each other and to the earth calls
for a new consciousness, a new symbolic culture and
spirituality.... We must see the work of eco-justice and
the work of spirituality as interrelated, the inner and
outer aspects of the one process of conversion and
transformation.* — ROSEMARY RADFORD RUETHER

All over the world and down through the ages the monastic and religious life has fostered values of simplicity and
frugality of lifestyle. The devotee sacrificed everything in
order to be unencumbered before God. And the vowed life
frowned upon those societal values of possessiveness, greed,
and the accumulation of wealth. Ironically, the monasteries themselves often became the most powerful and wealthy
institutions of the contemporary world.

The vow of poverty is meant to be the safeguard against
all abuses related to wealth and property. But in many cases
it is dogged by an underlying double flaw: (*a*) the accompanying spirituality is not about responsible care of the goods
of God's creation, but about stripping away all attachment to

material things so that the soul is set free for eternal life or for *nirvana;* and (*b*) the onus is ultimately on each individual person; consequently, the collective wealth (and abuse) of the monastery or community was never subjected to the same intensity of evangelical scrutiny.

Here we encounter the first major violence of the vow of poverty — one we encounter in all three vows — the dualistic division between person and culture, between the individual and the collectivity, between the human and the planetary. It is the violence of dualism, also the violence of fragmentation, creating the separation and isolation that breed so much alienation in the world of our time.

From Stewardship to Mutual Sustainability

Reclaiming the vows in their primordial meaning is a long and arduous task. The vow of poverty, as traditionally understood, emphasizes the betrayal of creation and the abandonment of basic human responsibility for the goods of creation entrusted to human care. True to patriarchal norms and expectations, the care of goods was entrusted to a hierarchical figure called the bursar or superior. And in classical childlike (or childish) fashion, we suppressed our adulthood and behaved with infantile submission.

Unknowingly, we colluded with the Judeo-Christian aspiration that we humans were to be the masters of creation, managers of the earthly order and its affairs. Mastery involves a quality of distance from what you are trying to master. There is no emotional attachment, nor indeed is their a spiritual one either. As an approach it has violence written all over it.

Many scholars have noted that the notion of humans as masters of the goods of creation does not occur in the New Testament. Instead, the notion of stewardship predominates. We are called to look after what is entrusted to our care, bearing in mind that we are doing it on behalf of someone who has given us use and usufruct in trust. Whereas "mastery" is a harsh and domineering term, "stewardship" has a feeling and caring connotation: "Blessed are the gentle for they shall inherit the earth" (Matt. 5:5).

In earlier writings (O'Murchu 1991, 1995), I suggested that we shift the emphasis from that of a vow of poverty to a vow for stewardship. My major reservation about that new naming, then and now, is that "stewardship" in both popular and biblical usage, envisages an "absentee landlord." In our case as a human species and as a Christian people, our God is neither absent nor is God a landlord, and we do violence to both ourselves and to God by continuing to resort to such imagery.

As creative people, called to discipleship with a cocreative God, we need to grapple further with the renaming of this vow. One suggested formula, a "vow for participation," has much to commend it. But my personal preference in the context of the present work is that of a *vow for mutual sustainability.*

In contemporary usage, "sustainability" encapsulates several important concepts that challenge the violence we are seeking to outgrow. Closely related to the word "sustenance," it reminds us that everything in life is gift given for nourishment and therefore not intended to be usurped or destroyed destructively. To sustain something in being requires renewed effort and devoted love, not the competitive or antagonistic behaviors that seek to undermine and exploit another. As used in ecological discourse over the past twenty years, "sustainability" highlights the complementary relationship of growth and the environment (see Burrows, Mayne, and Newbury 1991). A strategy which seeks the maximum output does not necessarily realize the optimum potential. Everything in creation belongs to a context and needs to be used in a caring and responsible way within the evolving nature of the context in which it is given. In the old understanding of the vow of poverty ownership of goods belonged to the community rather than to the individual.

This often led to widespread abuse and a great deal of irresponsible evasiveness. The notion of sustainability requires each and all of us to reclaim a real ownership of the goods entrusted to our care. The word "ownership" has a paradoxical ring to it. It oscillates between the possessiveness that all too quickly becomes a ferocious consumerist greed and our human temporality which time and again reminds us that we really own nothing. However, as we strive to adopt a nonviolent way of living, especially in our relation to the goods of creation, a spirituality of nonpossessive owning becomes quite an engaging vision.

The liminal witness then switches to a deeper level of reality whereby we religious, like all other humans, do own certain goods and have primary responsibility to protect and use them in a caring and sustainable way. It is in addressing the very practical question of *how* we use them that our liminal calling comes into focus.

Sustainability in its true meaning has mutuality built into it. However I add the qualifying adjective to highlight the cooperative and egalitarian sense of coresponsibility to which all humans are called at this time. We own nothing for exclusive personal use, nor does anybody have a right to claim exclusive use over anything in creation. Everything is gift — to be shared and used for mutual benefit. And because everything is gift, the liminal engagement entails a great deal more than shared use. Gifts are given first and foremost to be celebrated, to be endowments which evoke enrichment and gratitude. They invite us into mutual participation which is as much about discerning the meaning of the gift as it is about its responsible and appropriate use.

The fact that this is a long way from how people generally regard their material and earthly possessions is precisely the point I wish to make. We exert extreme violence upon our world and its giftedness, because we are so alienated from the created order. Our often felt human alienation or sense of being people in exile is much more about our estranged relationship from creation rather than from God. Our inherited tradition of being masters, or even stewards acting on behalf of an absent landlord, has left us bewildered and confused in our relationship to the world around us. We suffer from a debilitating sense of cosmic homelessness.

Reclaiming the vow for mutual sustainability is very much about coming home to ourselves as planetary-cosmic creatures who owe everything we are and everything we have to the creation out of which we have evolved. The earth is not an object given for our sustenance, or even for our delectation and delight. No, it is the primordial womb, which under God begets everything that exists, including ourselves. Our vocation to mutual sustainability is about learning afresh what it means to be at home where we really belong and to be at home creatively with all those others with whom we share the earth as home.

Reclaiming the liminal perspective highlights the destructive reductionism to which we have subjected all the vows. The legal minutiae and supercilious antics which we invented in the name of perfectionism virtually stripped the vows of all sense of global and earthly engagement. The vows are first and foremost centers for value radiation fostering the unfolding of the New Reign of God upon our earth. They were never intended to be individualized ascetical feats for the salvation of individual souls.

Ethical Ownership

The vow for mutual sustainability asserts that all forms of ownership have ethical consequences. Ownership is not a thing we do but a set of values we live out in daily life. Everything entrusted to my care is not merely a gift from God; it is also the fruit of creation and, in many cases, the creative expression of human ingenuity and struggle. What I choose to do even with the most basic of life's gifts has far-reaching implications for person and planet alike.

Ethical behavior is behavior informed by wisdom and eco-justice, just as unethical behavior tends to bear the marks of ignorance and poor self-awareness. How we regard the goods of creation and how we relate to them very much depends on how aware we are of the larger, even global, context in which these goods have significance — in themselves and for human beings. The consequent attitudes and actions regarding ownership will be affected by the quality of my awareness. And it is the wisdom arising from this awareness — or lack of it — that will determine whether I exercise that ownership in a way that moves toward mutuality, sustainability, and justice or toward self-aggrandizement.

The enlightened wisdom I have in mind is elucidated vividly by Joan Chittister (1995, 139):

> To say that we can possibly minister to the poor and never read a single article on the national debt; to think that we can be moral parts of a global community and never study a thing about the Third World debt; to imagine that we can save the planet and never learn a thing about ecology; to infer that we work to promote the women's issue but never go to a women's conference, read a feminist theologian or spend a minute tracing the history of ideas about women; to say we care about the homeless dying and never say a thing about the evil of homelessness or the lack of medical care for the indigent, smacks of pallid conviction at best. Simply to do things is not enough anymore. Professional education that fits us for particular skills but neglects to prepare a person for dealing with the great questions of human life is not enough anymore. The world needs thinkers who take thinking as a spiritual discipline. Anything else may well be denial practiced in the name of religion.

It is not a question of being an expert in every field of learning, nor is it about the accumulation of university qualifications — achievements which often spawn on the information-saturated world which perpetuates ignorance rather than the quality of enlightenment I allude to. I refer to a disposition of heart and attitude of mind which ultimately are qualities "given" with the liminal vocation itself.

In coming home to ourselves as people called to inhabit the liminal space, we realize that our vocation is to think the unthinkable, speak the unspeakable, bring to silence the raucous din of patriarchal verbiage and bring to word the subverted groans and imposed silence of the downtrodden and oppressed of our earth. To fulfil this task we need to be people who are informed on what is going on; we need to take time to read and reflect; we need frequent updating — in all that concerns the human search for meaning in life; finally, we need not one but several forums where the process of reflective dialogue transforms information into knowledge and knowledge into that wisdom which awakens the heart and begets new life.

The gross abuse of the planet's resources arises primarily from a debilitating ignorance about the meaning of creation and our human role within it. Apart entirely from spiritual considerations, our patriarchal dominance of the earth, along with the economics and politics that foster that dominance, is doomed to ultimate catastrophe. We are engulfed in a dark and frightening ignorance. Unless wise people are forthcoming, the future looks perilous indeed. Unearthing that wisdom and translating it into an engaging narrative for our time is a primary challenge for those committed to the vow for mutual sustainability.

A Passion for Justice

Ethical sustainability thrives on a wisdom that shakes and disturbs. It begets a quality of awareness and action which knows that, under God, things should be different from the way they now are, that God never intended forms of ownership which divide and alienate, which incarcerate and exploit people and their planet. From this restlessness is born the passion for justice without which the vow for mutual sustainability is merely a farcical facade.

As a biblical term "justice" is a prescriptive rather than a descriptive term. We religious often talk about justice and the need to work for it in a more creative and consistent way, but a quality of engagement that confronts the oppressive suffering of our time tends to elude us.

The dualism of the sacred and the secular violently undermines our potential to work for justice. The injustices that underpin so much barbarity and suffering in the world are essentially political and socioeconomic in nature and can be confronted only from within a sociopolitical context. Church prohibitions on religious inhibit many from more direct involvement in those political processes that could begin to confront the sinful injustices in the contexts where they really belong and through modes of engagement that would highlight the need for equity and equality in the world.

We also need to outgrow the restrictive religious connotations of justice-ministry. Justice is not just a notion that belongs to church or formal religion; it is a critical dimension of what makes relationships — at every level — sustainable or destructive. Today we use terms like "eco-justice" (Hessel 1996) or "geo-justice" (Conlon 1990) to describe the essential connection between the personal and the ecological, the spiritual and the earthly, aspects of our call to be justice-makers.

What is under review here more than anything else is our understanding of ourselves as human beings. Burdened by the violent and lopsided anthropocentrism of the past, we view ourselves as a species that has the right to dominate and control everything in the world. In our essential nature, however, we are an integral dimension of the created world. We are a cosmic-planetary species. And we can never hope to be in a right and just relationship with ourselves or with other people until we also engage with the justice issues that pertain to our ecological home, Planet Earth.

Our situation is further complicated by the long moralistic

tradition that attributes sinfulness and suffering to people's individual misdeeds. All sin is assumed to be personal and thus the proposed remedy of personal conversion is seen as the solution to all ills. This is another rendition of the patriarchal will to divide-and-conquer, which is itself the root of many violent injustices in today's world.

All the major religions are notoriously naive and ignorant about the systemic/institutional nature of sin and suffering in the world. The root cause of much injustice is not the unjust deeds done by individual people, but oppressive social and institutional forces that compel people into acting immorally and even oppressively of each other. In many parts of our world, governments themselves are the most corrupt and corrupting of influences. And the mainstream religions are not without their internalized oppressions, often fostering the values and strategies of war, sexism, exclusion, and patriarchal domination.

Most of our work for peace and justice, while nobly intended, is mere tokenism. We give generously to the poor of the two-thirds world, but by that very deed exonerate governments from having to address what is primarily a political problem. From within an ecclesiastical context we highlight the plight and oppression of millions who are denied basic human rights, but we don't speak our prophetic words to those who really perpetrate the crimes. And the perpetrators are often the first to remind us that our "preaching" belongs to the realm of holiness and that we should not be dabbling in political affairs. The justice that arises from the liminal space needs to be much more porous and transparent. It requires a set of skills and wisdoms that our traditional formation has never known. It requires a resilience and courage that is at one time profoundly spiritual yet imbued with a wisdom of how the world operates. It is a risky undertaking and its power is in the paradox of its engagement. And it is not an undertaking for lone individuals. It requires the ambience, support, and discernment of a group or a supportive network.

Fortunately, we can draw on some inspiring models to animate and guide us, ones the religions and churches often look at askance, because they perceive them to be on the wrong side of the secular/sacred dualism. I again allude to movements like the Campaign for Nuclear Disarmament (CND), Greenpeace, and the several feminist and ecological movements that are helping to shift consciousness in significant ways in the world today.

There is little doubt that it was the persistent and unrelenting efforts of groups like CND that eventually created the consciousness that could tumble the walls of hatred and suspicion and thus pave the way for the end of the Cold War. Their contribution to a more peaceful and safer world has rarely been recognized.

Similarly, Greenpeace, probably the single most liminal and prophetic movement in today's world, known, admired, yet detested by virtually every government on earth. This is a movement that knows what's going on, that understands the ecological threat that hangs over our world, that is radically aware of the collusive and oppressive policies of governments and other international corporations that undermine the sacredness of our earth and its creative potential, that works for justice through practical action but especially through a quality of consciousness-raising that is immensely practical and spiritual at the same time.

Greenpeace, in terms of its individual members or as an organization, does not use edifying or theological language, but it does that quality of action that begets justice and liberation, that helps to realize in today's world the radical possibilities of the *Basileia* which is at the heart of our Christian faith.

To be more effective as agents for gospel justice and liberation we religious need to translate into action many of our noble ideals about collaborative ministry. We need to collaborate with people and with movements that will make a difference to the quality of life on earth, and not merely to affairs within the church — many of which offer little hope for the urgent questions facing the world to-day. We need to develop a vision of networking — with agencies and organizations committed to transformative jus-tice — that invites us out of our narrow ecclesiastical confines into the real and more engaging world where the values of the New Reign of God confront those of suffering and oppression.

An authentic engagement with justice, more than any-thing else, characterizes our new understanding of the vow for mutual sustainability. In fact, many religious around the world engage afresh with the liminal implications of this vow. In recent years several orders and congregations, having become aware of how mainstream banks exacer-bate the pain and suffering incurred through Third World debt and also of how the banks contribute (at least indi-rectly) to the arms trade and other questionable projects, have decided to invest their monies elsewhere. Ethical invest-ment is a relatively novel idea, but one that many religious life groups have adopted as a integral dimension of their financial policies.

Internally, we are a great deal more enlightened on how the processes of injustice operate in reference to the very ba-sics of our sustenance and livelihood. We realize that it is not just a contemporary fad to purchase ozone-friendly and biodegradable household goods; it is a small but significant gesture of justice promotion, as is the manner in which we recycle waste and attend to its disposal.

Much more significant is the growing awareness of the jus-tice implications of the food we purchase and consume — an issue that is also expanding our awareness on how poison-infected our environment has become under the influence of patriarchal progress. At this level of awareness the con-nection between justice and nonviolence becomes all too apparent, and the need to ground our understanding of the vowed life in a spirituality of nonviolence becomes the only authentic liminal option.

Mutuality and Inclusivity

The ownership we religious profess questions the very foundations of contemporary political and socioeconomic order. It challenges all notions of private ownership from the realm of the human person right through to Planet Earth and the cosmos itself. It begins with the basic conviction that God has bestowed all life — and all life forms — for the mutual enrichment of the whole. God's creativity knows neither boundaries nor limits, and neither should humans' response.

From the liminal perspective of the vow for mutual sustainability, anthropocentrism is the most deadly sin of our age. It is the arrogance and self-inflation whereby humans set themselves up as masters of creation and proceed to lord it over other species, over nature, and, inadvertently, over God too. It is the compulsive masculine urge that seeks to divide and conquer everything it encounters, vividly and barbarously expressed in the oft-quoted words of Francis Bacon: "We must keep torturing nature 'til she reveals her last secrets to us."

It is this human addictive streak that holds the world to ransom. It is this insatiable power that some ten thousand years ago began the process of fragmenting Planet Earth into nation states and ethnic, racial groups, thus stripping humanity of its radical freedom to be a people of the whole earth with the planet as home. It is this hoarding addiction that led to the exploitation of the earth and its enormous resources leading right up to our own time in which the earth is ravaged, its resources are desecrated, and its peoples are plunged into depths of alienation and despair that we have probably never encountered in the four million years we have inhabited the home planet. We suffer from unprecedented levels of cosmic homelessness in which our bruised and battered earth is leaving us, too, sick in body, mind, and spirit. We are an integral dimension of the earth and what we inflict upon the creation around us ultimately comes back to haunt us. Unless, and until, our mutuality can include our cosmic and planetary sense of belonging, then all the patriarchal religion on earth will mean very little. And not surprisingly it is dying a timely death — and so indeed, it should!

As a Christian concept, mutuality also entails a radical quality of inclusiveness, particularly of those pushed to the margins of unsustainable means and therefore consigned to degrading levels of poverty and deprivation. It is not merely a question of greater fellowship, friendship, and sense of belonging. Nor is it merely the more inclusive and heroic acceptance of those marginalized because of economic or social status, race, gender, of personal or cultural difference. The need to include the proverbial "tax-collectors, prostitutes and sinners" at the table of Christian fellowship is a challenge many of us have yet to meet. But the radical inclusiveness goes a great deal further.

The starting point, however, need not be global or grandiose. Liminal possibilities often stare us in the face right where we are. What do we do when a woman is denied a post of responsibility simply because she is a woman? Why do we continue to collude with a church that excludes remarried divorced people from the eucharistic table? Why are we slow to denounce the homophobia that excludes people with HIV/AIDS from so many jobs and other social opportunities? Why do we continue to vote for politicians who support the maintenance of wine lakes and grain mountains in a world where half of humanity lives on the brink of starvation?

The mutuality of our vowed state knows no boundaries of exclusion. Yet, even the principles of private property have bored their way into our own way of life; we claim exclusive use of property, cars, and even bank accounts. We render unstinting service to the poor, but frequently at a safe distance from our own living space, sometimes expensively protected by high walls, the latest electronic alarms, and glaring neon lights.

The ancient distaste of the world is rarely spoken aloud these days, but it still permeates our way of being and our style of living with a deadly virulence. We are not at ease in our world, nor with its peoples, except when we are in charge. We say and preach nice things about vulnerability, but few of us manage to practice it integrally in the real world where people know the pain of exclusion and deprivation. Our ecclesiastical status imposes upon us a type of respectability which, more than anything else, undermines our liminal availability. It is difficult for us even to be as radically inclusive as Jesus was.

Little wonder then that the "preferential option for the poor" has been such a stumbling block for religious the world over. We know in our hearts that we are called to a quality of solidarity with the poor and marginalized that would leave us in a precarious and vulnerable space. Not only would it strip away all our comforts (that we could endure); what is much more problematic is the type of marginalization that might ensue in terms of my family, my friends, maybe my church (since many poor people no longer look to church or religion for hope) and above all those who hold me in "respectable" view. And instead of addressing our fears, we sidestep and rationalize them by resorting to heady questions like: Who are the poor anyhow? What poverty are we talking about? Are we not all poor in some sense? Does Jesus mean material poverty or spiritual poverty?

In fact, Jesus never talks about poverty, and he certainly does not commend it as something to be embraced, spiritually or materially. Jesus talks about the poor, not about poverty. And from a gospel perspective, the call and challenge for all humans is to work toward a new world order where poverty can be overcome and eventually eliminated. The message of God's New Reign — centered on the key values of love, justice, peace, and liberation — is the ultimate answer to the predicament of the poor of our world and to the deprivation wrought on creation itself by human exploitation. This vision includes the earth itself; nothing is excluded, since holistic inclusiveness is a precondition for the right relationships envisaged by Jesus in promulgating the vision of the New Reign of God.

The Poor in Spirit

All three vows have suffered from spiritual suffocation. We have so spiritualized the living of the vows that we have stripped them of their earthiness and their humanness and hence their capacity to serve the articulation and living out of archetypal values. We have portrayed a public image of the vowed life as a life of frugality and destitution. Frugal it might often have been, but not destitute. In many cases it was, and continues to be, a life well protected from the insecurities that the bulk of humanity has to live with everyday.

This false security we often explained away in spiritual rationalizations. Foremost among these was a call to be totally poor before God, dependent on God for all things. The emphasis often veered toward emptying oneself out, as Jesus allegedly did, becoming nothing so that God could become all in the depth of one's soul and spirit. Many harsh and self-inflicting penances were imposed and endured to attain that state of emptiness, that state of inner purity that guaranteed the soul its best chance of ultimate salvation.

Attempts to justify such extremes tend to focus on the prevailing culture of the time and the dominant understanding of the Christian faith within the cultural norms of the day. What is much more apparent today is the terrible and frightening reductionism that prevailed in earlier times. To accommodate the dictates of patriarchy everything had to be reduced to a manageable package, and everything including people was subjected to regimes that guaranteed power and control for those in charge. A spirituality of dualism and reductionism provided the divine veneer, the impression that we were trying to abide by God's will in minute detail.

Soul and not body became the primary concern. In this case "soul" refers to the realm of spirit which enlivens the body in the first place and departs from it in death. It was considered to be that part of the person that was really alive, and the only part that could fully attain union with the divine. More accurately, what we are dealing with here is spirit, not necessarily in its biblical pneumatic sense, but as the perfect dualistic opposite to the sinful materialistic body of the human and the earthly domain.

In the process of this evolution we lost touch with a much more ancient sense of soul, one that we are beginning to reclaim in the more open and holistic culture of our time. The vow for mutual sustainability is very much about the re-discovery of soul in all aspects of our daily life, especially our relationships with the goods of creation. It is this relationship of nonpossessive attachment that enables us to experience the blessings attributed to the poor in spirit whose radical availability to God automatically means a richly endowed participation in the unfolding Reign of God characterized by justice, love, peace, and liberation. Being poor in spirit is not a precondition for entry into God's New Reign; it is about participation in the process of its unfolding and growth.

Thomas Moore (1992, 229, 304–5) offers us the following description of en-souled living:

> The history of our century has shown the proclivity of neurotic spirituality toward psychosis and violence. Spirituality is powerful, and therefore has the potential for evil, as well as for good. The soul needs spirit, but our spirituality also needs soul — deep intelligence, a sensitivity to the symbolic and metaphoric life, and attachment to the world. . . .
>
> To the soul, memory is more important than planning, art more compelling than reason, and love more fulfilling than understanding. We know we are well on the way toward soul when we feel attachment to the world and the people around us and when we live as much from the heart as from the head. We know soul is being cared for when our pleasures feel deeper than usual, when we can let go of the need to be free of complexity and confusion, and when compassion takes the place of distrust and fear. Soul is interested in the

differences among cultures and individuals, and within ourselves it wants to be expressed in uniqueness if not in eccentricity.

Whereas the vow of poverty took detachment as a primary virtue the vow for mutual sustainability is built on a spirituality of attachment that cherishes the sacredness in the most simple of things and sees sacredness within complexity and even within confusion. A religiosity of detachment strips incarnation of its fleshiness and earthiness and undermines those en-souled relationships on which the New Reign of God is made possible.

The "poor in spirit" are precisely those people who are open to receive from the generous abundance of God because they know God to be radically near, immersed in the ordinariness of daily event and encounter. Embraced by this unconditional love, even our pathologies become the stuff of soul, raw material for growth into wholeness (see Moore 1994, 209–29).

The vow for mutual sustainability calls us to more soulful living, rediscovering the sacredness within and without all living things. We are called to befriend both the ordinariness and complexity that characterize reality. We are invited to embrace the "polytheism" (Moore 1994, 66) of diversity that must never be reduced to any patriarchal "monotheism." And perhaps most important of all, we need to redeem the power of imagination which awakens the reverberating creativity that shivers within every aspect of life.

The vow for mutual sustainability is more about being rich in soul rather than poor in spirit. Archetypally, the meaning is essentially the same, but the language we now employ must be one that liberates us from the oppression of the past in order to engage us with the liminal task of demolishing competitive consumerism and replacing it with a politics of care and compassion.

Under God, the whole earth is ours and yet nothing is ours. All is entrusted to our care, to develop and re-create.

Yes, all is ours, but in a cocreative relationship with the God who walks with us and among us. In the engaging words of John O'Donohue (1997, 180):

> In the world of creative work, where your gift is engaged, there is no competition. . . . In the world of soul, the more you have, the more everyone has. The rhythm of soul is the surprise of endless enrichment.

Perhaps the peoples of Paleolithic times were the most soulful of all our ancestors in regarding the earth as the body of the Great Mother Goddess. Never would they dream of hurting or damaging the womb that begets and sustains everything that exists. Intuitively, they knew what mutual sustainability was all about. We are the ones who have strayed and lost the deep wisdom. It is up to the liminal people to revive it. And time is of the essence — if we are to have an earth upon which to walk lovingly and gently once more.

CHAPTER FIVE

The Violence of Patriarchal Control

> The world does not depend upon us, and the world is not available to us. The world is out beyond us in God's wisdom. It mocks our pitiful efforts at control, mastery, and domination. — WALTER BRUEGGEMANN

> A monarchical God who rules from a distance, controlling the world through domination and benevolence, supports anthropocentrism and androcentrism as well as promoting both human passivity and social models of domination and submission.
> — SALLY NOLAND MACNICHOL

Patriarchy is a word which occurs frequently in the pages of this book. In its popular meaning it refers to the masculine will-to-power that tends to adopt the strategy of "divide and conquer." It is a virulent force that dominates the contemporary global scene of governance and order, often subverting and undermining the complementary values of feminine creativity, passion, and freedom.

Historically, we can trace its origins to the upsurge of the Agricultural Revolution some ten thousand years ago, although it was some thousands of years later before its impact became significant. Prior to that time, we humans lived in a totally different relationship with the planet, with creation at large, and with each other in the more holistic and egalitarian relationships which seem to have prevailed in those ancient times.

The transition from pre-Agricultural to post-Agricultural times is complex, and our sources are speculative rather than factual. Life before agriculture was far from idyllic, and the subsequent development of a more masculine orientation certainly brought benefit and progress. We are dealing with a complex mixture of light and shadow. To date, historians exalt the light (the progress) and tend to underestimate the shadow, the frightening price we have paid for that progress. My concern in this reexamination of the vow of obedience is the long-ignored shadow and its impact on all structures of authority down to our own time.

Patriarchy and Religion

The cultivation of the land, the sowing of seeds, and the production of crops marked a massive leap for humankind. It birthed a new realization of the potential of the soil and the benefits it could accrue for humanity. What quickly became precarious was the strategy on how best to dole out those benefits to the satisfaction of all. One way to do it was divide up the land and parcel it out to prospective cultivators. It sounds fair and reasonable until a more conscientious producer needed extra space. We can assume there were some ancient bargaining procedures to procure the extra land, but greed became uncontrollable and eventually you fought for what you needed. Warfare was born and became the tool of patriarchy for many subsequent millennia.

Today, it is difficult to envisage the perceptual gaze of the people who lived in pre-Agricultural times. You walked out of your hut (if you had one), stood on the earth, and the whole creation was yours for as far as the eye could see, and far beyond it. There were no boundaries, nation states, or ethnic minorities. All was one, and everything belonged to everybody.

A great debate unfolds today about the spiritual understanding of those ancient peoples (see O'Murchu 1997b).

They certainly had a sense of faith, and the evidence we
have suggests that it was deeply rooted in the surrounding creation. A growing body of evidence also points to the
universal worship of God as woman, whose body was perceived to be that of the earth itself. The earth was sacred, a
prodigious womb for sustenance and support. There seems
a distinct possibility that the people understood life as a cooperative coexistence within the nourishing womb of Planet
Earth itself.

The reasons for the rather sudden shift to the agricultural
way of life are complex and as yet poorly understood (see
Mithen 1996, esp. 217–26) and are not immediately relevant to the considerations of this chapter. Once the shift
began to happen, the attitude toward and appreciation of
the earth as a fertile womb also changed quite dramatically.
The earth came to be seen as an object to be conquered
and controlled rather than as an organism with a prodigious
potential for life.

And the influence of the Mother Goddess, whether imag-
ined or real, seems to have been a hindrance that the
patriarchal powers were determined to get rid of. They began to develop a spirituality of sky gods, male gendered,
strong and powerful, reinforcing the prototypical male on
earth. At this stage, the image of the one Great Goddess
was being fragmented into that of several minor goddesses,
which occurs in many of the great Eastern religious traditions. This development was countered by the patriarchal
notion of monotheism. There was to be only one God, a
king-like male, a divine father who ruled and controlled from
on high.

What men did on earth God did in the heavens. That was
the original perception. It was only a matter of time until
the notion of the sky god became more fixed and permanent
and he became the one that validated everything the male
patriarchs deemed necessary to exercise power on earth.

And then religion was born. Formal religion as we know
it today dates back to about 3000 B.C.E. Many historians,

reading history with the limited and jaundiced view of patriarchy, go along with the idea that this is the first time God makes a unique intervention in history. They misread the whole scenario and conjure up some bombastic theories of divine deliverance. It may have been a time of special divine disclosures, but we are on much surer ground in unearthing yet another ploy of patriarchy's indomitable urge for control: religion itself was a device to control the power of the god(s) which patriarchy itself had invented.

What we are encountering here is an enormously complex and confusing development between religion and spirituality, a topic I have explored at length elsewhere (O'Murchu 1997b). Spirituality is endemic to the human species; increasingly, we encounter evidence to suggest that a spiritual will-toward-meaning is innate to creation at large. But most people consider spirituality to be an offshoot of religion. Religion comes first, then spirituality.

This is one of the great deceptions of patriarchal power. Religion as a system which seeks to generate and protect human meaning is percolated through and through with a will-to-power. Not the power of the divine, but of the human beings who set out to conquer and control the whole of reality in post-Agricultural times.

Spirituality, for which we can glean anthropological and historical evidence, going back to at least 70,000 B.C.E., is a much more egalitarian concept. It is a wisdom shared by all people, a wisdom that searches and seeks out the meaning of life. Like religion, spirituality has its sacred personages, chief among them being the shaman (or shamaness). The shaman was highly revered, but never exalted on high to the same degree that the priest was in later times. Although there was a hereditary factor involved, shamans could function only when they were called forth by the people and missioned into the sacred task. And among the shaman's primary roles was that of healer and not just a mediator between the divine and human realms.

As I indicate in an earlier work, the shaman may be

considered to be the prototype for the ancient monk and for all those who subsequently respond to the call to the vowed life. Theologically this seems to be a much more fertile line to access the significance of the vowed life rather than aligning ourselves with the vocation of priesthood, a connection which has had some retrogressive consequences for both the theological and cultural meaning of the vowed life. Among these is our collusion with the power of clericalism, which more than anything else has determined the traditional understanding of the vow of obedience.

Violent Subjugation

The vow of obedience operated on the understanding that there existed a chain of command from the ordinary member up to the local superior, then to the provincial, superior general, pope and, ultimately, God. It was an exact replica of the military chain of command — even using military language like "general" — and was often designed on a military model.

Because God was the one at top of the ladder, there was an unquestioned assumption that every thing that was "commanded" down along the line was a perfect representation of God's will. The person receiving the command could neither disagree nor dissent, and, true to military fashion, if one did indicate any disapproval, one was stigmatized for a long time afterward. The external disapproval often became an internal wound that had horrendous consequences, particularly for female religious.

Today, we experience in religious life a massive sigh of relief as that cruel, barbaric burden is being lifted off our shoulders. If only that were true universally! In many parts of the Catholic world, the old system continues unabated, albeit in a modified form. Many Sisters in Africa live under the bondage and oppression of dictatorial bishops, while all over the world subtle pressures are brought to bear on leadership personnel to "tighten things up."

Religious all over our world struggle as they try to loosen up and humanize the oppressive systems we have inherited from the past. A great deal of liberation still awaits us, but not until the healing touch of life enables us to transcend the past and turn our eyes and hearts to a more wholesome future. Central to that future will be a fresh view of our vowed commitment, with a much more radical resolve to live and work nonviolently at the liminal spaces of the contemporary world, a world weary of war-games and power-struggles, a world hungering for the enduring and sustaining power of the divine *shalom*.

The problems which the vow of obedience poses for us religious — and the destructive violence it generates — go right back into the misty and murky origins of patriarchy itself, hence the rather long exposition at the beginning of this chapter. We need to acknowledge and appropriate that fact before we can begin to purge and purify ourselves of its oppressive erosion. It is not just a problem of a male-dominated church which we think we can begin to rectify by closer cooperation with the clergy, better dialogue with the local bishop, or rewriting *Mutuae Relationes,* a set of guidelines issued by the Sacred Congregation for Religious to facilitate dialogue and harmony between religious and the church's hierarchy. All these strategies amount to little more than tinkering around with a sick system that needs radical surgery.

And from the liminal perspective, we need to remind ourselves that the goal of our endeavor is not the vowed life itself, but the whole earth-human community for whom the liminal people exist in the first place. In naming the sins of patriarchy, particularly from the stance of outrageous prophesy (see Daly 1978, 1992), it is the whole of God's creation and all God's people we are seeking to liberate. Within religious life itself we cannot hope to obtain creative and authentic freedom until all God's creatures (human and nonhuman alike) are set free within the cocreative interdependence of universal life.

The Vow for Mutual Collaboration

It is a strange irony, and a great surprise for some, that the word "obedience" itself embodies many of the sentiments expressed above. The root word, *ob-audiere,* means to listen attentively. It requires a radical and attentive openness to the deeper message and meaning of all that we are asked to attend to. Only in the light of such deep listening can we respond in a more wholesome way.

That quality of response is the precondition for the liberation that the Christian Scriptures allude to over and over again. It is a freedom *for* rather than a freedom *from,* a freedom for that fulness of life promised by Christ and indeed by all the great spiritual leaders of the various faith traditions. With that creative freedom as our central focus I suggest we rename the call to obedience as *the vow for mutual collaboration.*

The tautology is quite deliberate. Collaboration requires mutuality as a central feature of all its interactions. Yet, because of the radicality of what is envisaged here and because of the enormous backlog of oppressive violence that needs to be undone, it feels important that the tautologous phrase "mutual collaboration" is retained.

What I am seeking to reclaim more than anything else is that we humans are primarily an altruistic, cooperative, nonaggressive species, whose fundamental spiritual and relational capacities dispose us to love life rather than undermine it. In other words, our tendency to be an aggressive, violent, and destructive species is largely, if not totally, the product of the patriarchal brainwashing of the past ten thousand years, and many of the major institutions in our world today — including all the political and religious ones — are the direct result of that misguided orientation.

These claims many will consider to be wild and exaggerated. They challenge and threaten the reductionistic, closed worldview which we consider to be normative and enduring. They force us to reexamine perceptions sanctioned by tradition and "divine certitude." We humans have walked this earth as a creative, divinely endowed species for over two million years (and that is merely in our capacity as *homo erectus*). Yet, 95 percent of that sacred story we have virtually eliminated completely from our consciousness because the stultified patriarchal imagination of the past ten thousand years has done everything in its power to subvert and erode it.

The reader needs to keep in mind that whereas ten thousand years seems almost incomprehensible to most people (again, because of patriarchal brainwashing) it is less than 5 percent of the time we humans have walked this earth. It does not reflect the larger, evolutionary reality of what it means to be human, a species endowed with the capacity to cocreate with our creative God. The other 95 percent of our story needs to be reclaimed if we are to understand more fully what our planetary and spiritual role is all about. We do justice neither to ourselves, nor to our creative God, to carve up and fragment our sacred story, subverting the greater part of it because it suits the deadly and deadening forces of patriarchy that have prevailed over recent millennia.

At this juncture I also need to reassert that I believe one of the primary roles of liminal people is to keep the big picture before our eyes, to save us, and our world, from the suffocation of minimalism, from the patriarchal reductionism that feeds the philosophy of "divide and conquer." The view from the liminal space looks out from the spooky realms of congested oppression; despite the blinkered and myopic view of our inherited "education," the eyes of our hearts are still undimmed. Our spirits reawaken as we gaze across God's creative landscape, the prodigious explosion of life which has prevailed over billions of years, and the unfolding human story that despite its current fragmentation yearns afresh for a more participative and integrated role in the unraveling mystery of human and planetary life.

As a species we know deep in our hearts that we belong to an evolutionary sacredness, which we struggled to engage with for at least sixty thousand years before patriarchy ensued. And during all that time, the growing body of evidence shows that we were not the savage and primitive exploiters the patriarchs try to convince us we were, but a largely benevolent, relational, and spiritually motivated species. We certainly were not perfect, nor am I in any way trying to depict an idyllic past; the facts seems to suggest that we rarely, if ever, behaved in the cruel and barbaric manner that depicts the five thousand years of "civilization." The age of barbarism, the power of patriarchy, had not yet evolved. Now that it has evolved and mercifully is beginning to crack at the seams, we need to reconnect with our more authentic selves, we need to re-member what it really means to be a cosmic and planetary human species.

Our capacity to behave mutually comes first and foremost from the fact that we are essentially a relational species. To foment the "divide-and-conquer" mentality of patriarchy, humans were deemed to be atomized units, independent individuals, whose ultimate identity could only be discovered and lived out alone before the world and before God. That rabid, competitive individualism still prevails, often leaving a violent trail of depression, alcoholism, and even suicide in its wake. Many still aspire to be the robust individuals who will vie for power and glory in the vicious game of patriarchal imperialism. Fortunately, growing numbers are beginning to suspect that it is all a great facade, based on a fundamentally flawed set of assumptions.

Basic to such assumptions is the false identity that has been imposed upon us; in a sense, we have imposed it upon ourselves. As modern psychology reminds us, we humans are at all times the sum of our relationships. Each one of us is a relational matrix, and therein lies our true evolutionary and spiritual identity. The capacity to relate is at the very core of what it means to be human. Our very existence is dependent on the mutual interaction of two people who brought us into being in the first place. And there is a growing awareness that the happiness and wholeness of my personal life very largely depends on the quality of love and intimacy that surrounds me, especially during my formative years.

Gradually, too, we are beginning to rediscover and reclaim our relationship with the earth, and indeed with the whole of creation. The fact that the carbon which forms the basis of all life, including human life, is itself the product of exploding stars is an elegant reminder to us of the interdependence and mutuality which underpins everything in our universe. We belong totally and completely to the universe we inhabit, and without it our lives are simply not possible. Consequently, the more alienated we become from the surrounding creation — a state instigated by the blasphemous dualisms of patriarchy — the more life becomes a hell on earth. Our relationality is at the basis of all our efforts and endeavors to live meaningfully in the midst of creation.

Consequently, hierarchical ordering, the birthchild of patriarchy, is fundamentally alien to human beings. Whether exercised politically or religiously, it deviates from, and diminishes, the human capacity to relate with that radical equality and egalitarian cooperation that belongs to our deeper spiritual nature. Our evolutionary history (apart from the ten thousand years of patriarchy) and our spiritual nature disposes us to be people whose growth flourishes when we interact collaboratively — around all the major issues that impinge upon our planetary-human existence.

Because of our conditioning over thousands of years and the erasure of our creative imaginations, it is painfully difficult for many of us to even envisage the scenario I am outlining. We have been cloned into being moronic, stupefied robots, lethargic and exhausted by the dead weight of the power from on high. The thought that it could be — should be — different, is almost too frightening to entertain. Frightening because the conditioning of the past has already scared us to the point of ossification.

But there is hope around, and it comes from the most outrageous of places, outrageous to those who assume that the hierarchical ordering is of God or at least put in place by "intelligent" human beings. But many don't believe in it any more; suspicion is becoming respectable these days and increasing numbers of people are brave and free enough to walk away from oppressive workplaces, debilitating relationships, insipid religions, and diabolical politics. Disturbing, I agree, is the vacuum being created, but that may be a necessary stage in the chaos that marks the disintegration of the old while we await a rebirth of something new and vital. Befriending that painful transition, naming its creative unfolding, and empowering people to stay with the chaos may well be the most urgent tasks for liminal people at this time.

Overcoming Intransigence

For those called to the vowed life, the shift envisaged in these reflections is dauntingly difficult. As indicated in previous chapters, the shift envisaged in the vow for relatedness (celibacy) and in the vow for mutual sustainability (poverty) is already beginning to take shape in our lives and in our convictions. When it comes to the vow for mutual collaboration (obedience), however, we are in quite a morass. On the surface, we operate a more consultative and collaborative approach, but at the formal level most of our structures and institutions are unmistakably hierarchical and any effort to alter these (e.g., superiorless communities, brothers assuming roles of responsibility in "clerical" congregations) meets with strong opposition from the hierarchical church.

Within our ranks a great deal of ambivalence prevails. Many people carrying the hurts of the oppressive past lead very individual lifestyles and find mutual accountability a burden almost too heavy to bear. People entrusted with leadership ministry spend exorbitant amounts of time consulting everybody about everything, often leading to an outcome of total paralysis. Meanwhile, the rising younger generations, perhaps frightened by the prospect of anarchy — for which they have been neither spiritually nor psychologically prepared — often hanker for the apparent simplicity and orderliness of the older approach.

It is a muddled and confusing landscape made all the more convoluted by the superficial theology of the religious life that has prevailed ever since the Council of Trent, when the vowed life effectively became an adjunct of the clericalized church. Not until we reclaim our liminal identity in a more explicit and vociferous way will we religious be able to engage with the major questions of meaning that our world invites us to address in this age — and in every age.

While we try to grapple with an intransigence of the surrounding culture, still clinging ferociously to the formal structures of patriarchy, there exists within our own ranks an intellectual and spiritual intransigence which is draining away our lifeblood. Fundamentally, this is the intransigence of formal religion itself, which ridicules and trivializes every effort to question its authority and authenticity. All hierarchical leaderships — secular or religious — are convinced that their access to wisdom and truth is grounded ultimately in a supreme authority. Not all will consider it divine in the religious sense, but they do regard its judgment to be based on ultimate truth and they consider its assertions to be beyond question, unless evidence to the contrary is glaringly obvious.

The concentration of power is central to the patriarchal understanding of authority. All the power becomes vested in the few, leaving the many devoid of power and also stripped of real opportunities to exercise responsibility. There is within every human being a creative urge, a power that comes from within. Only in a culture of mutual collaboration can this creativity be tapped — to the benefit of all creatures and to the mutual advancement of life in its evolutionary grandeur.

Today, the vast majority of people are disempowered, not just in one, but in several significant ways. This leaves our human world with an enormous waste of God-given creative giftedness; it potentiates frustration and violence; it breeds dissipation and despair. It is a sacrilege not merely against God, but also against humanity itself and against the planet we inhabit.

Embracing Collaboration

Collaboration essentially means a readiness to relate and work in cooperation and harmony, maximizing the diversity of gifts and talents that belong to the entire body of participants. It does not require an external source of imposition; in a world striving to be in tune with deeper archetypal values, it is the most natural and creative way for humans to live and behave.

The capacity to relate belongs not merely to each one of us as individuals; it is also an endowment with which we are blessed collectively. Cooperation and not competition characterizes the human species, a conviction that is difficult to claim in a culture saturated with dissension, strife, rivalry, and combat. And worst of all, this scenario is normalized and validated in the name of the ruling god(s) of patriarchal religion.

The vow for mutual collaboration, therefore, is not just about exercising authority in a new way and in a more egalitarian fashion. It is much more about a conversion of heart and mind that allows and enables us to see life differently. It is about seeing with the evolutionary eyes of our human story in its wholeness and not in the fragmentation and decimation wrought by patriarchal recklessness. It is about seeing with the critical eyes of wisdom and suspicion that will not accept at face value the oppressive perceptions of patriarchy. It is about seeing with discernment and seeking the guidance of a God whose wisdom and judgment far exceeds the religious "truths" of the past five thousand years.

The liminal implications of mutual collaboration involve speaking truth to power, surfacing afresh what has long been subjugated and stating anew what has become virtually unspeakable. As Mary Daly (1992, 136) warns (in reference to the pursuit of women's liberation) this is a quality of seeing that will evoke huge resistance:

> It is understandable that most men would prefer not to see. It is also understandable that many women would prefer not to see. Seeing means everything changes; you can't go home again. It is not "prudent" to see too well. Therefore, the ethic emerging in the struggle for women's liberation has as its main theme not prudence but existential courage.

The voice of prudence veers toward the practical necessity of somebody having to be in charge; otherwise, things never get done. The voice of prudence also tries to be reasonable; it suggests that despite all its limitations, the present model has stood the test of time and deserves another chance. The voice of prudence can be subtle, and even devious, in admonishing the transformation of what already exists rather than creating the dangerous power vacuum that could reap havoc.

Prudence does not mix well with liminality. There is no such thing as a prudent "cutting edge." Nor indeed is there anything prudent in the Jesus who gathered tax-collectors and sinners around the table of intimate, spiritual fellowship and advocated that we call no one on earth our father. Prudence belongs to that ascetical spiritual climate of *apatheia*; it has no place in the pathos that is engendered by the prophetic imagination.

What Daly calls "existential courage" is the courage to see the whole picture of our living context and to reclaim it as our true home. It is the courage to let go of the patriarchal, anthropocentric props that tried to set us up as the masters of creation and then in typical duplicity accuses us of being victimized by original sin. It is original patriarchy and not original sin that is the source of our problem.

Our alienation from self, God, and creation arose from the abuse of power and not from some convoluted divine flaw. It is we who invented the cosmic flaw and not God; by the same token it is up to us to rectify it, and that is essentially what the call to mutual collaboration is all about.

The existential courage to perceive and conceive differently is also the wellspring of those creative and collaborative resources whereby we feel the need to act differently. Humanity today cries out for a more participative way of being. Far too many people have been railroaded into helplessness and deprivation of spirit. Even the few governments of our world which prize themselves in being radically democratic and talk all the right jargon about human rights and planetary well-being thrive on the shoulders (and wealth) of the few who have power and successfully delude the passive millions with a sham semblance of "making a choice" at the ballot box. In fact, millions have already opted out, as is apparent in the last three presidential elections of the United States when a meager 50 percent of the electorate came out to vote; the other 50 percent saw no point. And those elected chose not to see the political malaise in which they are surrounded, one that could erupt into extensive violence in just a few decades from now.

Religious often deliberate about their own lack of involvement in the life of the church or about their concern for the people who also feel marginalized. From a liminal point of view, we must never reserve our concern merely to the church, because what's happening in the church is merely a reflection of what's happening in the world at large. We must cast our gaze on the larger reality and on the deeper causes. Liminality involves depth, and anything short of the total picture is a betrayal of our liminal calling on behalf of the people who invoke in us the liminal vocation in the first place.

What precisely does the vow for mutual collaboration entail in terms of structures for authority and leadership within the religious life itself? At the present time, in this age of transition, it invites us to a willingness to explore and experiment. The blueprint, if there is one, is not about structures but about consciousness. We need to open wide the eyes of our hearts and see beyond the congested strictures that dictate the suffocating structures of the contemporary world; then, and only then, can God really disturb us and evoke from us the existential courage to walk away from the "empty tomb" and embrace the tenuous and risky hope of what God's creativity will make possible in God's own time.

The courage and creativity to make this existential leap itself will beget the evolving shape of what the call to mutual collaboration is about. None of us can traverse this existential journey on our own; apart from being too scary, it requires the support and dialogue of others for genuine discernment to take place. Those three words, "support," "dialogue," and "discernment," already tell us a great deal of the practical structuring of the vow for mutual collaboration. What we must not collude with is a "more collaborative" way of operating the hierarchical system. There is nothing absolute or divinely inspired about this system. It is a man-made artifact that advances and enhances male, patriarchal power. Like a garment that at one time might have been useful, it has worn thin; it is beyond patching; it has outgrown its usefulness and should be discarded.

Because our imaginations have been in bondage for so long, we confront suggestions of patriarchy's demise with the fear-filled allegations that all hell will break lose and anarchy will reign supreme. Yes, indeed, it will if we choose to remain in mental and spiritual paralysis, blind to the fact that such anarchy is already rampant despite all the "law and order" of patriarchal (mis)management.

The collapse of patriarchal control and its cherished hierarchical structures does not in itself create a world of chaos and confusion. It is the subversion of human creativity and the erosion of feminine power that begets the human and political paralysis that leads to ennui.

We humans are creatures who search for and pursue meaning. We are social beings who over the millennia have invented, time and again, structures that facilitate creative, personal, social, political, and ritual interaction. Sometimes these structures are distinctly hierarchical in nature; the difference is that they have arisen from human initiative in a culture where the dynamics of fluidity and creativity prevailed, thus guaranteeing that the structures did not become rigid and unwieldy.

Increasingly we also realize that forces of nature, beyond our human control, rescued us from our intransigence, often demolishing "sacred cows" that we thought would last forever. And the creative drive of evolution, which never seems to lose the accumulated wisdom and energy of the past, pushes us on to new and unprecedented horizons. Indeed, it may take a cataclysmic event of evolutionary proportion to rescue us from the logjam of patriarchal imperialism, from which it seems well nigh impossible to disentangle ourselves on the conscious level.

The call to mutual collaboration is a call to a new quality of global participation. It is a new way (in fact, a very old way) of engaging with our cocreative God at the heart of the world. Whether or not the Christian Church, or any of the major religions, adopt this new strategy, is of no great consequence. We are dealing with larger, more engaging questions pertaining to the human family across time and culture. And it is the breadth and scope of this wisdom, the emerging consciousness of our time that must engage liminal people more than anything else.

The liminal vocation, with its call to mutual collaboration, is about a global shift in consciousness. It is the new way of seeing and perceiving that will beget new action. Let's direct our energy to where it really matters; let's direct our resources to where they'll make a real difference. Let's reclaim the liminal horizon that points us to exciting possibilities filled with the hope and promise of a new tomorrow.

CHAPTER SIX

Learning to Relate Nonviolently

Innocence does not consist in simply "not harming."
This is the fallacy of ideologies of non-violence. Power-
ful innocence is seeking and naming the deep mysteries
of interconnectedness. — MARY DALY

Obscene is not the picture of a woman who exposes her
pubic hair, but that of a fully clad general who exposes
his medals rewarded in a war of aggression; obscene is
not the ritual of the hippies but the declaration of a high
dignitary of the church that war is necessary for peace.
— HERBERT MARCUSE

The option for nonviolence is not just about acting in a different way. Even if we brought an end to the warfare and political violence in the world today, people would still behave violently toward each other and toward the planet we inhabit. This observation leads many theorists to assert that we are innately violent and will always be that way.[9] That conviction in itself almost spurs us into further violence. The cycle never ends.

We do violence to the notion of violence itself by construing its evolution according to the delusory perceptions of patriarchal research. Whether we adopt the encapsulation theory of Marie Balmary, the seduction theory of Jean Laplanche, the tragedy theory of Alphonse de Waelhens, or, best known of all, the victimization theory of René Girard (all outlined by O'Shea 1996), we fall well short of that comprehensive view which helps us to unearth the deeper and more ancient causes of the violence that surrounds us.

All these theories draw liberally on the Genesis story of Adam and Eve in the Garden of Eden, which they interpret as a primordial experience of alienation setting people in antagonistic relationships from the dawn of time. They interpret Genesis with a naive and grossly misleading literalism. Not a single theorist (that I am aware of) situates the story against the background of the Agricultural Revolution, which I suggest is the primary reference for the "expulsion from the garden" that preoccupies the writer(s) of the book of Genesis.

To resolve the violence, as understood against this background, scholars like Girard give elaborate attention to the need for a cultural scapegoat (see the comprehensive commentary by Bailie 1997). For Girard, the Christ of Christianity is the supreme example of such a scapegoat. Once again, we encounter a dangerous and misleading literalism in which Jesus is construed with the individual personalism of all other human beings (and his archetypal, cosmic significance is not even mentioned), and no attention is given to the patriarchal context which influences Christianity — along with other world religions — into being a powerful force of validation for the violent domination of patriarchy itself.

It is this collusion with violence which is inscribed in the very fabric of formal religion that makes the liminal option for nonviolence so difficult for contemporary religious. The vowed life has been so coopted (a respectable violent strategy) into mainstream religion that it has lost virtually all semblance of the alternative counterculture it is called to embrace on behalf of humanity and our planet. Reclaiming our liminal space will not be an easy task.

A New Way of Relating

Three important realms of experience require special attention as dimensions of our unfolding story. There is the reality

1st

we take for granted, that understanding of our reality —
and the vows — which the formal institutions consider to be
normative, and therefore should remain unquestioned. That
stance in itself breeds violence, the alienation, oppression,
and reaction that arises when the imagination is muted and
the lifestyle becomes suffocating.   *2nd*

The second important realm is the experience of transition
that is inescapable in our time. Within the Catholic Church
all experimentation in our living of the vowed life was to be
complete by 1980, and with the promulgation of new consti-
tutions it was assumed that things would return to normal.
In fact, it was only in the 1990s, with the serious demise of
many orders and congregations, that the full impact of transition began to hit home. The pain and challenge of being in
transition is now a great deal more real.

Times of transition carry their own type of violence. It is
not so much the alienation we experience as the fear of being able to speak openly to it and the dread that we might
be castigated for doing so. The suppression of grief — the
need to mourn our historical, cultural, and religious past —
is another violent act, with serious consequences for both
individual and group. And the various inhibitions against
experimental action — which of course poses a threat to
"stability" and "normality" — ultimately reap destructive
fallout rather than constructive possibilities.

3rd The third realm of experience, the one our whole planet
is trying to make sense of at this time, is our yearning for a
different future, our ambivalence about it, or even our resistance to it. In all cases, there is an intuition that something
different is in the air. In some quarters, there is the tendency to throw everything overboard, discard the past in its
entirety, and opt for a totally new future.

There is a kind of violence here, an uprooting that leaves
us at the mercy of all types of unknown forces. The main
problem here is how we understand tradition and how we
circumscribe the ignorance of patriarchal research which always segregates us from the deep wisdom which we need to

sustain us in times of transition, and which is our greatest resource in dreaming alternative possibilities for the future.

We are dealing with three different ways of relating. Relationships are the clue to the nonviolent way we are exploring in this book. I therefore attempt a resume of the relational dynamics that belong to the living out of the vows at the three levels outlined above. The table on page 104 illustrates the journey we are called to traverse from the previous, and still dominant, understanding of the vows (our past), which I deem to be fundamentally violent, to the untidy transition which many religious experience today (our present), to the nonviolent aspirations for a new and different future.

The material in the first and second columns is easier to comprehend because it relates to lived experience of the immediate or distant past. The material in the third column is an attempt at naming the values that undergird the nonviolent approach to life. Central to such values are relationships, the most authentic cultural and spiritual context for living the vows today.

Sustainability Revisited

We begin with the vow for mutual sustainability and review the features named in the left-hand column. In this context, the vow denotes nonattachment and deprivation as preconditions for availability to, and total dependence on, God. The assumption is that attachment to material and bodily aspects of life distracts from our commitment to God. Underlying the assumption is the conviction that God and godliness is dualistically opposed to all material and created form. The contingency of created forms is perceived to be not merely inferior to the divine but is also somehow contrary to the purposes of the divine.

Because of this dualism of the sacred vs. the secular, a perpetual state of internal conflict is invoked. The interrelationship of body, mind, and spirit is undermined. The wholeness that underlies our human existence is forever being reduced to a state of fragmented agitation. We end up almost telling God that s(he) should never have created us as we are.

The material destitution that characterized this way of life is undergirded by an even more destructive spiritual destitution which I name "deprivation of soul." Holiness tends to be portrayed as a distrust and suspicion of creation, including the human body. Rarely, therefore, if indeed ever, do we connect with the sacredness of the ordinary, with the soulfulness of simple things, with "incarnation" as it blooms in the ordinariness of so many daily events and experiences.

Inevitably our relationships become precarious, destructive, and violent of self, others, and creation at large. A climate of codependency often ensues, whereby we expect others (especially the superior, bursar, etc.) to carry out duties and responsibilities on our behalf; meanwhile, we sometimes sink unawares into an apathetic trance of irresponsibility and may seek to validate it as providing more time and energy for the things of God.

The "stripping away" for which the old understanding of the vow is reputed has no place in an incarnational faith like Christianity. The God being worshiped is a caricature of the patriarchal will to dominate, subdue, and control. The whole construct is violently destructive. And while we may wish to forgive our forebears for promoting this value system and successfully explaining its appropriateness for the culture of the time, we can never accept it as genuinely Christian or indeed authentic according to any of the religious aspirations of the great world faiths.

Not surprisingly, therefore, the center column in the table on page 104 is entitled "ambivalence." This is the transitional space in which some — and not necessarily the older members of our orders and congregations — lament the heroism and simplicity of the past, while others rage (internally and sometimes externally) at the victimization that *law*   *Vows for Nonviolence*   *value*

VIOLENCE	AMBIVALENCE	NONVIOLENCE
Poverty	*"Cluttered"*	*Mutual Sustainability*
Detachment	Confused expectations of self and others	Stewardship
Deprivation of soul	Burdensome and unclear	Nonpossessive ownership
Irresponsible caring	"Who, now, is responsible for what?"	Coresponsibility
Managing with what we can quantify	Ideological shift: from heroism to trust	Goods entrusted to us by God
Dualistic divisions, e.g., spiritual vs. material	Difficult integration	Befriending the material creation
Destitute, yet very secure	Difficult to let go of old securities	Living simply so that others may simply live
Perfectionism by "stripping away"	Shift in spirituality	Holiness via wholesome sharing
Celibacy	*Reclaiming Sexuality*	*Relatedness*
Disembodiment	My *body* / My body!	Embodiment
Asexual	Shame – promiscuity	Pan-sexual
Mechanistic conditioning	Facts of life vs. Values for living	Archetypal contextualization
Suppression of feeling	"How far can I go?"	Engage with your feelings
Denial	"Afraid to tell you who I am"	Acknowledgment
Repressing the shadow	"Opening a can of worms?"	Befriending the shadow
Avoid temptation	How much risk ...	Take the risk of relating
Keep your vow	"Even if I am unfaithful?"	Live your liminality
"Stay in the closet"	"Coming out is best"	"Be true to your *whole* self"
Obedience	*Ineffectual Democracy*	*Mutual Collaboration*
Power	Requires new skills	Service of mutuality
Hierarchy	"Fine in theory, but ... "	Community
Shirk responsibility	Much ambivalence	Shared responsibility
Superior/inferior	Seeking an illusive balance	Mutual partnership
Divine/Patriarchal certitude	"How do we do it?"	Search through discernment
Structured institutions	Fear of disintegration	Networks
Teaching	Conflicting sense of allegiance	Listening
In the name of the church	Paradigm shift	In the name of the *Basileia*

ensued. Trying to live out of the old value system has left
many religious severely damaged in their incarnational integrity; in reaction many have left religious life in the hope
of reclaiming what they lost over the years.

The middle column is where we also detect an impatient,
at times reckless, desire for a better future. Honoring this
hunger requires sensitive discernment and a great deal of
dialogue. In part the impatience is conscious but probably
substantially more subconscious. From deep within we are
driven by a hunger for what we know deep in our hearts to
be a more authentic and Christ-like way of engaging with,
and participating in, the world of daily life.

The column on the right requires little commentary. It lists
some of the key features which lead to the renaming of this
vow as the vow for mutual sustainability. This requires the
fullest possible participation from every member of a local
or intentional community. This new vision is not based simply on a need to be more egalitarian; it is firmly rooted in
the vision of the *Basileia,* with its personal, interpersonal,
and global sense of responsibility. It is the way that leads
to the *shalom* that Christ prayed for, not some idyllic sense
of unperturbed harmony, but a proactive mobilization of all
our gifts, put at the service of God's own gift of creation, in
order to fashion the "new creation" and contribute to the
unfolding of the *Basileia* on earth.

Relatedness Reclaimed

Scanning the three columns of the renamed vow for relatedness, the left-hand column is very much about the violence
of denial. The prevailing culture was predominantly one of
disembodied living. And since sexuality was perceived to be
primarily a biological process for the purpose of procreation,
the denial of the body inevitably led to widespread repression
of our sexual giftedness. As already indicated in chapter 3,
the consequences have been quite destructive; one wonders if

even a word as strong as "violence" adequately describes the trail of destruction that has ensued.

The overspill becomes apparent in the polarized struggle outlined in the middle column. Among contemporary women, we detect a fierce protectiveness of their bodies — in case they might be snatched away from them again. For some, it tends to become a type of narcissistic preoccupation with the "body beautiful" (hence the statement "my *body*") in which the body can assume a disproportionate importance compared to other dimensions of the personality. Another significant strand, one often associated with the pro-abortion lobby, places the emphasis on the fact that it is *my* body, implicitly denouncing the patriarchal control of the female body, especially over the past few hundred years.

What the middle column illustrates more than anything else is the tension between the oppressive sense of shame inherited from our excessively moralistic past and the re-active urge to move toward the opposite extreme of sexual acting-out and a tendency to adopt promiscuous behavior. The internal turmoil and confusion of mind and spirit may feel overwhelming at times. Throughout the 1960s and the 1970s many celibates, upon leaving religious life, rushed into relationships which quite quickly became sexualized. Although many of these relationships have endured, they have not been without their share of pain and anguish; the unresolved issues of the past continue to haunt and to disturb.

Others sought refuge in psychotherapy — the forum where many of the "quoted" statements in the middle column are first articulated — and for some this has been a process of reintegration covering several years. More painful than the personal process of growth has been the frustration of try-ing to reintegrate into mainstream religious life. The capacity to connect, disclose when necessary, dialogue, and reinte-grate, facilitated within the therapeutic context could not — in many cases — be continued in the communities in which many people sought reentry; in some cases, the dysfunctionality, for both the individual and the community, became even more apparent.

Appropriating a sense of sexuality being about values rather than biological processes (the third column) has, in fact, been liberating and growth-enhancing for many religious. And these women and men, although often struggling within their congregational settings, can offer extensive healing and growth, in their apostolic ministries. What often becomes apparent is the surprising discovery that the psychosexual dysfunctionality experienced within the vowed life is proportionately no different than that encountered in the human population generally. In fact, many religious struggle in exemplary fashion with issues of psychosexual growth and this empowers them to be creative catalysts at the liminal cutting edges of today's sexually confused world.

Such people already embody and witness to the "wholeness" of incarnational living. It is not a question of being perfect or never deviating from a life of total integrity. Rather it is about the awareness of who we are as psychosexual people blessed with this highly volatile and explosively creative capacity which forever seeks outlet and expression in authentic relatedness, a vision lucidly explored in Moore (1998).

An incarnational, holistic view of human sexuality also acknowledges that it can never be reduced to merely a biological or psychological process. More than any other aspect of the human personality, our sexuality touches upon and awakens archetypal values. Our erotic drives and desires are not merely genital, or simply aimed at interpersonal behavior; they belong to the same universal energy that creates and begets new life across the aeons. The sexual attraction is itself a dimension of the curved space that pushes all life forms toward union and communion. Not without good reason has human eroticism been described as a dimension of the divine delirium.

Viewed archetypally, sexuality is an embodied energy, yet never located in any one erogenous zone, nor merely confined to the realms of embodied encounter. We employ the term "pan-sexual" to describe the locus of psychosexual energy as dispersed throughout the entire body, but also capable of being awakened and invoked by sensory input from many sources of nature and of life. The mystical state is particularly susceptible to sexual fantasy and arousal. Traditionally, this has been interpreted as evil temptation to distract the devotee from the things of God, a perception that begins to change when we acknowledge that God is also the creator of sexuality and of the erotic creative energy that gives birth to stars and humans alike.

Collaboration Reinstated

Issues involving authority and leadership usurp a great deal of time and energy within religious communities today. This is partly due to the ambivalence or indifference which these issues often evoke. Many people bring into the vowed life unresolved authority issues from their families of origin. Many are adversely affected by the competitive brainwashing of early schooling and education. This leaves some hungering for power, and others feeling totally powerless.

"Power" is the key word to understanding the material in the left-hand column; indeed, power undergirds much of the violence we are seeking to address in this book. It is a power validated in the name of formal religion and contextualized within the structures of the institutional church. In its extreme form, it is considered never to be in error or in doubt. It is a closed system which resists any attempt at evaluation and will always seek to disempower those who question its meaning or validity.

Because many people feel so powerless in the face of such a system, the shift away from this focus tends to be marked by apathy and indifference. This is manifest in religious life today in the increasing difficulty to find anybody to assume a leadership role. On the other hand, everybody expects to have a say in the process of discernment and decision-making. We end up with what I call "ineffectual democracy" (second column) wherein everybody expects to be consulted about every issue. This often leads to a paralysis of inaction, and sometimes to a power vacuum in which abusive forms of dominance and control are exercised by those who hold no formal positions of authority and sometimes also by those who do. A group can often feel trapped in fear and inertia.

Not everything in the middle column is necessarily negative or destructive. Several contemporary groups experiment with alternative ways of sharing power and resources. The enthusiasm is often eroded, not for want of trying but rather because of the cynicism of those who wish to hold on to the old forms. And growing numbers are beginning to reclaim a sense of their personal power and are striving to discern more creatively where, and where not, to place the little power they feel they have. It is for this type of positive reason, rather than out of negative motivation, that a substantial number choose not to get involved in maintaining the patriarchal structures still required by canonical and ecclesiastical governance.

The major — and at times subtle — shift in the vow for mutual collaboration is from the definitive nature of organized structures (institutions) toward more loosely affiliated networks, characterized by trust and mutuality (third column). This is not democracy in some new veneer. Networks work because people want them to work; they draw on the diversity of unique gifts and talents, attending (listening) to each person's wisdom and insight and discerning an outcome for the benefit of the whole group or enterprise.

In the Christian context, the *Basileia* is the ultimate and definitive model for all networks. The table fellowship from which no one is excluded is the contextual paradigm, and the Beatitudes, which declare blessed the very ones whom the patriarchy of the day dismissed as unimportant, is the blueprint for the networking approach. In the service of mutuality, based on trust and the calling forth of many gifts, more egalitarian ways can be found for partnership and collaboration.

The new paradigm may feel vague and fuzzy, precisely because this third vow, more than the other two, has been left largely unexplored. The weight of patriarchal tradition lies heavily upon us, and the intransigence of patriarchal power is virtually impossible to shift. Often, the only way out is to hope and pray that it will run its course and die its timely death, sooner rather than later.

Laws and Values

The left-hand column takes law to be the ultimate guide to authentic living. The right-hand column envisages value as a more fundamental criterion. I juxtapose these two concepts in order to highlight the transition we are exploring. It is not my wish to create yet another false and meaningless dualism.

The function of law — religious and otherwise — is to protect freedom. Therefore, law itself is primarily a value rather than a set of legalistic guidelines. It is precisely when those who make and seek to implement law forget or bypass its primary purpose that priorities become confused. It is then that the biblical directive — the law is made for the person, not the person for the law (Mark 2:27) — gets lost in the legal maze.

Basic to all other values listed in the right-hand column is the capacity to relate. This I understand to be the primordial wellspring of meaning on which everything in the universe, including our growth in faith, is based. Evolutionary theory, quantum physics, and contemporary spirituality all point to the same fundamental source (see O'Murchu 1997a, esp. 65–90). The very structure of time-space, one of curved arches and not of straight lines, is a permanent divine imprint reminding us that even at a geophysical level everything in the universe is intended to encounter everything else. This is the nonnegotiable that must never be compromised.[10]

Although religion, in the very etymology of the word, seeks to connect and unite, and every religion claims to be about the formation and growth of community consciousness, this original inspiration has always been usurped by the structures and institutions the religions have adopted. All follow a hierarchical system in one shape or another; all have colluded with forces of power and domination; all have adopted linear rational mind-sets, and, most disturbing, all have contributed to violence and destruction in the world.

Politically, socially, economically, and religiously, the aspiration for a new world order wins laudable approval. Everybody seems to want it, yet it continually eludes us. The confusion rests in the fact that we think we can bring about the new vision from within the old structures. There is a fundamental contradiction in a patriarchal system seeking to promote egalitarian, communal values. Morgan (1989, 51) succinctly states the problem:

> If I had to name one quality as the genius of patriarchy it would be compartmentalization, the capacity for institutionalizing disconnection. Intellect severed from emotion. Thought separated from action. Science split from art. The earth itself divided: national borders. Human beings categorized: by sex, age, race, ethnicity, sexual preference, height, weight, class, religion, physical ability, ad nauseam.

The two sets of values are so radically opposed it is well nigh impossible for them to coexist. Hierarchical value systems of their very essence breed inequality; some have power over others; some are considered better, wiser, holier. In a patriarchal system there are always winners and losers. In the Christian vision of the *Basileia,* the patriarchal losers have the first place at the table of fellowship; while the religions seek to exclude the "unworthy," Jesus requires us to grant them a primary space of inclusion.

The capacity to relate knows no boundaries. The whole of creation is included, with the vast unknown realms of time-space as yet undiscovered by humans. And those volatile, creative dimensions of human life, e.g., sexuality and our untidy emotions, must also be included and related to anew. Everything in our world is interconnected. We must outgrow the violent enforcement of fragmentation, separation, and division, whether done in the name of national politics, regional economics, or different religions. What unites us is far more powerful and godly than what divides us. It is to our own peril that we ignore this timely message.

The liminal witness, therefore, centers on relationships more than on anything else. The vowed life is about plumbing the depths of our interconnectedness as a cosmic, planetary, and personal species. Our primary vocation is global and universal and should never be subjugated to the norms or laws of any one political or religious system.

Our accountability is to the entire people of the earth, and this too has cosmic and planetary dimensions. Confining the vowed life to religious enclaves is an act of blasphemy. It flies in the face our relational (Trinitarian) God who missions us to the creative fringes where our call is to keep pushing and transforming the boundaries that undermine authentic relationships. No realm of life is beyond our concern. We do not have to be experts in everything or, indeed, in anything. The wisdom we witness to is a wisdom of the heart, and while it does require the human tasks of learning, reflecting, and sharing, ultimately it belongs to the unlimited giftedness of the wise and wonderful God who calls us into being in the first place.

For many religious today, this may seem a daunting and impossible undertaking. Breaking through the domestication of the vowed life over several centuries — indeed five millennia if we include the experience of the other major religions — will not be an easy task. Perhaps we can each begin by trying to break through the sacred vs. secular dualism in which many of us are spiritually and humanly trapped. Can we reclaim in all its fulness the invitation to be an incarnational people called to follow the global Christ of the

Basileia? And can we strive to break out of the narrow confines of that spirituality that focused on individual salvation and allow our hearts to be touched by the God of unconditional love who unceasingly sends us to our brothers and sisters at the heart of creation?

The whole world is held in the embrace of the God of unconditional love. We, too, as cocreators with that creative God must hold our world — totally and lovingly. Only a vision as large and as deep as this can help to heal the scars of our violent destructibility. Only in working for right relationships, characterized by love, justice, peace, and liberation, can we undermine the violence of separation and division which, even today, is far too prevalent across our suffering earth.

CHAPTER SEVEN

Beyond the Collusion with Violence

Violence is so inherently fascinating that it distracts us from the more fundamental mechanisms that underlie it. — GIL BAILIE

Sacred violence provides the state with its legitimacy and fuels the optimism and idolatry of the patriot. It sanctions the judiciary, justifies class distinctions, bestows prestige on the "best people," and dignifies the executioner. — ROBERT HAMERTON-KELLY

Scarcely a day goes by in which the newspaper or our television screen doesn't display acts of violence and terror. Sometimes the images are too much for our gaze; we turn away in horror or in denial. Or we stare in numbed attention, gripped by crippling despair because there is so little we can do about it all.

We admire those who work for peace, who negotiate reconciliation, whether between unions and workers or between warring nations. We join networks that promote justice in the world. And we try to do what we can in our own neighborhood. Something in our hearts and perhaps also in our faith tells us that every effort makes a difference, and cumulatively we hope we are contributing to bringing about a better world for all to live in.

But, then, disaster strikes! Not a devastating earthquake or some freak storm of nature, but the news that a reputable politician is charged with massive fraud, a high-powered businessman is named as the chief culprit in an international drugs cartel; a multinational company in the United States has been exploiting millions in the two-thirds world for over ten years; a European state has been shipping armaments to Burma to kill and maim those who struggle for basic rights.

Our hopes are shattered! Painfully, we begin to see what we are up against. The people "at the top" that we had long trusted, the guardians of law and order, those in whom we had placed our hope, have let us down. And it has happened so often in the past few decades we know that corruption and injustice are rife. Yet, ironically, we continue to vote for these people, and purchase their goods, and even advocate the sale of weapons of destruction because our employment depends upon it.

The central point I wish to make in this chapter is that we all collude with the violence that reaps havoc on our planet and on our lives today. And it is this dark and sinister collusion that poses the greatest challenge to liminal witness. We cannot hope to bring about a world of justice and love until we address the banality in which we all collude.

Our Deluded Anthropocentrism

The violence we seek to address is not innate to human beings. This is an academic patriarchal delusion which very successfully distracts from the real problem. And all the religions swallow the pathetic logic while wasting enormous resources of time and energy perpetuating a cult of individual guilt. Individually, many of our politicians and representatives of multinational corporations are people of dignity and integrity, but, caught in the web of dysfunctional systems, they betray even their own deepest values. It is not individual culpability but systemic sin that underpins the moral malaise of today's world.

There are several layers to "the system," but basic to all of them is the unquestioned assumption of the patriarchal value system that life is there to be conquered and controlled and that it is our right and duty as human beings to do the dividing and conquering. The very language used is heavily militaristic. Creation is set up as an adversarial, objectified entity and under the influence of formal religion is denounced as secular, superficial, and, in some cases, evil.

Anthropocentrism is at the heart of the problem. In the words of Collins (1995, 18): "We take ourselves and our needs as the focus, norm and final arbiter of all that exists." We assume that we are the only ones who are fully alive, that proportionately everything else is less alive, and that the earth itself — trees, lakes, rocks, minerals — is dead inert matter. And occasionally we justify our insatiable desire to divide and conquer by invoking the command in Genesis 1:26–28 to be masters of creation with the destiny to subdue and cultivate the earth.

In another work (O'Murchu 1997b), I explore briefly the anthropological and paleontological foundations of this worldview, which for many people (and scholars) is presumed to have existed since time immemorial. In fact, it seems to be quite recent (in evolutionary terms), dating back over the past ten thousand years to the dawn of the Agricultural Revolution. Prior to that time, not everything was right in how we humans related to the earth or to each other, but in general we seem to have related in a more connected and holistic way. Increasing evidence suggests that our collusion with violence, destruction, and an adversarial relationship to the created world is very much a development of post-Agricultural times.

In terms of our self-understanding it seems essential to underscore two controversial claims:

(a) Our tendency toward violence is a cultural acquisition rather than an innate predisposition;

(b) For well over 90 percent of our time on Planet Earth we humans related with each other and with the wider dimensions of planetary life in what was fundamentally a nonviolent manner. The allegation that our prehistoric ancestors behaved in a barbaric and savage manner is a projection from the present onto the past. In the long history of the hominoid species, we, of recent millennia, seem to be the most violent that has ever existed.

Our propensity for violence is not just behavioral, but more fundamentally perceptual. We tend to view life at every level in minimalist and utilitarian terms. We perceive ourselves as superior to every other life form and set ourselves up as adversaries to the rest of creation. We solemnize dualistic divisions and disconnect ourselves from the interdependent relationships which are fundamental to all life forms. And then we wonder why alienation is so prevalent; it is we ourselves who have invented it.

The long journey home to our true selves — which is what the vowed life is all about — must begin with perceptual conversion. We need to begin by addressing our cultural blindness, that myopic veneer of normalcy which is driving us all mad. We must open wide the eyes of the heart and see ourselves in the full planetary and cosmic dimensions of our existence. Only then will we truly understand who we are meant to be. Only then will we truly understand the folly of our patriarchal manipulation.

Having taken that initial step we will begin to accept — with humility and forgiveness — the several ways in which we have colluded, and continue to collude, with violence. We'll begin to see the cruel contradiction of trying to secure peace by amassing weapons of mass destruction; we'll begin to understand the outrageous blasphemy of invoking God's blessing upon weapons of warfare; we'll begin to realize that the power we validate in the name of the supreme sky god is a monstrosity not of God but of our own making; we'll see that the world of formal employment, where human creativity is victimized by financial productivity, destroys the vision of the human soul; as we reconnect we'll begin to realize that the dualisms that helped us to manage the world, now leave us saturated in fragmentation and alienation.

To resolve our deluded perceptions we need to acquire a deeper sense of wisdom. We are bombarded with knowledge and information (see Kaku 1998), but without the wisdom that can discern the deeper meaning and forge the more holistic connections, the information explosion becomes yet another target for the misguided drive to divide and conquer. The Gulf War of 1991 was fought more on the basis of strategic information than with strategic weapons. Crime prevention on both national and international scales is forever chasing the sophisticated mobilization of underground information. The misuse and abuse of information is itself one of the most violent activities in today's world.

Language and Metaphor

We glimpse the disturbing landscape of our concern by noting the violent nature of ordinary daily discourse. We allude to the "battle" for survival, against cancer, against racism, against unemployment. All our dominant relationships are construed in military terms. Almost unknowingly we are forever "fighting." And we wonder why peace in our troubled world is so elusive! The answer is obvious.

We also suffer from an epidemic of "reports." We roll out "white" papers and "green" papers, "position statements," and "strategic planning." We analyze the parts to death, while the whole continually eludes us. We swim in a deluge of facts and figures which confound rather than enlighten us. Our heads are cluttered, and our hearts are disconnected.

To cope with the impact, we talk about "downsizing" the system — which in fact rarely leads to a more comprehensible understanding. The compulsive need to quantify and objectify often leads to a suffocating minimalism. Our mechanized approach to information management — using computers, the Net, the Web, etc. — fails to connect us meaningfully to the wisdom that underlies universal life.

Although many disclaim and feel we have outgrown the

metaphor of "man the machine" (which we tend to associate with the Industrial Age), something much more sinister has happened to us. The alienation of the Industrial Age related more to the power machines had over us, a type of external pressure we rightly questioned and resented. Today we suffer more from an internalized form of oppression whereby we have allowed ourselves to become robot-type agents in the mechanized technology. The language we use to describe mental states and genetic processes becomes increasingly more mechanical and alienating. Our relationship with the "web" of information makes us hungry and gullible rather than enlightened and at peace. More than ever before we are caught up in a rat race where we feel more like victims than real participants. We are engulfed in an alarming sense of estrangement.

What I describe, of course, is a phenomenon of the wealthy and powerful one-third world, largely unknown to the impoverished suffering people of the two-thirds world. Even where the poor of the earth are acquainted with what's going on, perhaps daily surfing the Web like everybody else, they are largely unaware of how we use that same technology to keep humanity divided into those who have and those who have not, those who exploit and those who are exploited, the rich and the poor. Sadly, the information explosion, despite all its promise of hope, is yet another way in which many of us collude with the violence of exploitation and oppression.

Naming Our Relatedness

We break through the collusion with violence by envisioning our reality in a different light. We need to reclaim the wholeness over the fragmentation and give priority to complementarity over dualistic divisions. We also need to learn ways and means of protecting our "fulness" against the erosive threat of reductionism.

As we develop a different set of perceptions, we will need

to rename our experiences afresh. We tend to identify many things by labels that distort rather than by names that protect and liberate potential. In all the formal religious traditions naming provides a mode of identification that releases potential for fresh possibility. In the Christian gospels, naming is a dynamic concept at the service of mission.

Mission today, whether understood spiritually or in some other way, must always embrace global horizons; otherwise, we once again fall foul of suffocating reductionism, insularism, competition, and violence. The ultimate horizon of all our outreach, and the core element in all our naming, is relationship. It is here, and not in atomistic isolation, that life at every level discovers its true purpose.

We come into being because of a relational matrix, and that is open to several different levels of understanding: scientifically, biologically, socially, and theologically. The purpose of our existence is to enhance and advance life's capacity to relate. An interdependent world knows no isolated enclaves. We humans need to start undoing the many we have created. And then we need to redirect our creative energies to where they truly belong: a mutually creative engagement with our relational God in a relational universe.

Breaking the cycle of violence also requires us to break the cycle of domination and the destructive codependency that often follows. Everybody is challenged to grow into an adult way of relating mutually and interdependently. As a species, the capacity to do this is written into our very genes.[11] The problem is that we have largely forgotten who we are; the brainwashing of the past ten thousand years has left us ambivalent and confused about our true nature.

The motivation to redress this complex identity problem is not just a human preoccupation. Many people do not even see the problem, and many of those "powerful" people to whom we look for guidance in life don't even want to know that there is a problem. (They are subtle and devious enough to know that it would threaten their power base). The motivation is more global than personal. The universe itself, and especially our desecrated and suffering earth, is crying out for attention. Because we ourselves are an integral dimension of creation we too "groan inwardly" for the new freedom to relate in a different way. Evolution itself is pushing us to new relational horizons.

Liminality and the New Horizon

These are exciting times for those of us called to live at the cutting edge. The brave new world that so many desire awaits our creative engagement. There is so much to be renamed and proclaimed! A new story is waiting to be told.

The theology of religious life that takes liminality as its central concept, its core value, invites religious to outgrow the limited and relatively safe institutions of the past few hundred years and move once more to where the vowed life really belongs: fresh horizons of risk, possibility, and hope.

It is not just any horizon, nor is it a conglomerate of fringe options based simply and solely on individual choice. We are alluding to evangelical options which in the best biblical sense are about the liberation of the poor and oppressed in order to release the new life of the *Basileia*.

Historically, religious men and women are at their best in seeking to identify and serve people in acute need, marginalized and disempowered by the forces of oppression. Increasingly, we feel called to include the earth itself in that circle of contestation and compassion. Because we are creatures of creation, we suffer when she suffers and we are liberated within her liberation.

In terms of the new vision explored in this book, the liminars of the vowed life are invited to activate and ground a shift in consciousness which has enormous implications for humanity and our future on Planet Earth. We are called in genuine prophetic fashion to denounce and lament the patriarchal values of the status quo which no longer sustain or invigorate. And we are challenged to dream alternative possibilities to the numbed powers and dysfunctional structures that weigh heavy on our shoulders today.

Specifically, the liminal vocation evokes in us some challenging and disturbing invitations to witness:

a. The old intellectual hegemony of male certitude which spawned the political-economic systems of the modern world is frayed at the seams. Its patriarchal will-to-power serves no purpose other than perpetuating the imperialism of the regime itself. We need to learn to lament and mourn its demise; only then do we become free to disengage and move toward new ways of engaging with our human and planetary reality.

b. The formal religions, which have long validated the value system of patriarchy, are also progressively disintegrating. Reviving or revitalizing the religions does not seem be an authentic liminal option. The religions may well have served their purpose. It is the rediscovery of spirituality rather than the recovery of religion that will preoccupy the liminal space for the foreseeable future.

c. With spirituality as our guiding light, relationships become a primary target of our concern and action. The American author Charlene Spretnak describes spirituality as "the aspect of human existence that explores the subtle forces of energy in and around us and reveals to us profound interconnectedness" (quoted in Raphael 1996, 226). All the vows address issues relating to the use and abuse of creative energy, whether invested in the goods of creation, in human sexuality, or in the human need for collaboration and mutuality. And in all three cases we need to outgrow the atomistic fragmentation of the past, along with the accompanying divisive dualisms, and move toward reclaiming the unity and relatedness that underpins all reality.

d. In promoting relationships as the central dynamic force throughout the whole of reality, we are seeking to change and reform a value system with a tradition of ten thousand years behind it. Not everything in that historical epoch was bad, but the prevailing values are clearly at variance with what the creative Spirit is seeking to awaken in our time. From the guardians of orthodoxy — religious and political — we will meet with much opposition, ridicule, and subversion. We may elicit surprising interest and good will from "ordinary" people, many of whom are quite disillusioned with the political, economic, and religious values that currently prevail. Our perseverance will largely depend on our prophetic resilience, the discerning support of those who deep in their hearts know what we're about.

e. I frequently allude to the political scene. The secular/sacred dualism and the church/state divide make no sense whatever to liminal people. I also wish to submit they make no sense within the biblical vision of the *Basileia*. Currently, it is our political systems (in collusion with multinational corporations) that dictate and control the prevailing values of our world — all of which are violent in one way or another. We cannot hope to change and reorient the values until we engage with the political-economic world. This may or may not involve joining political parties; in general, the liminal engagement tends to veer toward grassroot networks rather than formal organizations, political or otherwise. The networks, being closer to the ordinary people, tend to reflect the real issues more authentically and creatively than formal organizations for whom self-enhancement is often the real goal.

f. The liminal view is also about reality writ large. The liminars must be keenly aware of the terrible destruction reductionism has done to our world and to our own species. Liminal witness will strive to remain open to several interpretations for every aspect of reality. No question is ever formally closed, because such closure is an act of idolatry and often an act of blasphemy. And the "God of surprises" will have a special place in liminal discernment, even the God who works creatively with chaos:

> The edge of chaos is where new ideas and innovative genotypes are forever nibbling away at the edge

of the status quo, and where even the most entrenched old guard will eventually be overthrown, ... where eons of evolutionary stability suddenly give way to whole-sale species transformation. The edge of chaos is the constantly shifting battle zone between stagnation and anarchy, the one place where a complex system can be spontaneous, adaptive and alive. (Waldrop 1992, 12)

g. As indicated previously, spirituality rather than religion fuels the liminal vision. Religious boundaries and the do-mestication imposed in the name of churches and religions hinder the search for holistic truth. Liminal witness seeks to unearth the sacredness that underpins every aspiration toward wholeness. In discerning the greater whole we en-counter the God who is totally within yet totally beyond all our conceptions, religious ones included. A new understand-ing of God, spirituality, and religion begins to surface; in fact, these are ancient subverted understandings, as I indicate in previous works (O'Murchu 1997a, 1997b).

Nonviolent Re-membering

As indicated in our opening chapter, nonviolence is not just about the absence of conflict and warfare, nor is it about an insipid harmonious collusion where we subvert conflict in order to be nice to each other all the time. Nonviolence promotes creative ways of speaking our truth in love and seeks never to sacrifice truth for the sake of love. It invites us to speak our respective truths and convictions in transpar-ent and nondefensive ways, to listen attentively to alternative views and opinions, and to acquire skills for constructive dialogue that engages each person and every viewpoint in striving to reach consensus or a meaningful compromise.

Motivating the nonviolent vision is the biblical notion of *shalom*. This is the peace that endures because it is the fruit of long, and at times tedious, engagement. It heeds the wounds of the past, the bitterness and the resentments of yesteryear, and it seeks to create conditions where reconciliation, forgiveness, and healing can begin to happen. Socially and politically, it adopts all the skills for dialogue and negotiation that have been tried and tested. But it never stops here; the *shalom* of God always points to a larger horizon.

That horizon stretches from the primordial foundations of creation itself, right through to the personal, relational story of each creature (human and otherwise) toward the periphery of the future where hope never dwindles. The *shalom* of God re-members every speck of dust that ever was or will be; in the depths of divine wisdom nothing ever was or ever would be separated. Mutuality is imprinted in the very fabric of space-time. In scientific language, "All bodies are endowed with a principle of mutual gravitation" (Crawford 1997, 211, n. 13).

Nonviolence is not something we do; it is not even an attitude of mind or heart. It involves a whole new way of being in the world, a relational mutuality that belongs intimately and integrally to creation itself and to every aspect of it. If original sin means anything today, perhaps what it should denote is the painful reminder to us humans that it is we, more than any other creature, who have fractured and betrayed the cosmic and planetary relational matrix — and that is the basis for most of the meaningless suffering and cruel violence that mars our world today.

It is we humans who have to start re-membering — putting back together again, in story, in action, and in ritual — the fragmentation of universal life that we have brought about. And the fragmentation we often feel within, will never be resolved until we address the fragmentation without. In the holistic worldview, the nonviolent view, the within and the without are one. Everything is interdependent; in biblical language, everything belongs to the covenantal relationship. Only by reconnecting what we have disconnected can we truly realize the way to salvation.

And when we choose to adopt the nonviolent way, hope will be born anew. Not the hope of salvation in some distant heaven, nor the hope that can be realized only by scapegoating some divine savior nailed to a cross in every generation. The Christ event reminds us that it is we ourselves who are nailed to that cross and it is we ourselves who do the crucifying. And God will not work some magical redemption for cocreative creatures who have been endowed to do it for themselves. As human-divine creatures we have been abundantly resourced to break the vicious, violent cycle and reclaim our true humanity reconciled to our world and to our God. The daunting question is: Will we take the risk and have the courage to do it?

But how can we expect the masses to do it if the liminal people don't unlock the nerve points that make it possible? As catalysts for this different quality of reality we have allowed our liminal power to be subverted and numbed. The prophetic voice has been drowned out by the din of fragmentation and the drone of empty verbiage. The liminal call of our time requires us to rediscover wisdom to enlighten our knowledge, discernment to transform our argumentation, holistic vision to transcend the patriarchal crave to divide and conquer, and the *shalom* of God to heal the bitterness and pain of our destructive fragmentation.

In short, the liminal vocation is a call to transform those behaviors and attitudes which cause us to collude with violence. Brueggemann (1993, 55ff.) provides a useful synthesis for that undertaking, one that serves as an appropriate conclusion to the reflections of this book. He names amnesia, greed, and despair as our inherited sins:

> *amnesia* with no memory of our astonishing point of origin,
>
> *greed, acquisitiveness, and idolatry* that assure a brutalizing present, and
>
> *despair* with no hope for our destiny or completion.

In our world of fragmented disconnectedness we encounter:

> *memory* in a community that aggressively forgets,

> *covenant* in a community enmeshed in commodity,

> and *hope* in a community that believes very little is promised or possible.

The counterwitness for which liminal movements are called to be the front line requires us to:

> *remember* a rich past in the face of entrenched amnesia,

> *entertain a covenantal* (read *relational*) present in the face of a regnant commoditization,

> and *hope* for a marvelous future in the face of an established, resigned despair.

The world awaits our response. Our history provides abundant evidence that we can rise to the challenge (see O'Murchu 1991, 1995). It's a time to wait in hope on our creative God, who in God's own time will bring us home to where we religious really belong: the new frontiers that offer hope and fresh possibility for the ever new manifestations of God's reign on earth. Homecoming, too, is what humanity today yearns for. Even the rich and powerful, who thrive on violent consumerism and aggressive competition, are not at peace with themselves nor with the world. The violent way is a pathway to nihilism, for rich and poor alike. The *shalom* of God calls us home to where we truly belong, in relation to self, others, and our creative universe. It is that homecoming more than anything else that must engage the vowed liminars of the future; to choose otherwise puts the liminal witness itself in perdition.

Notes

1. I borrow the concept "archetypal" from Jungian psychology. Basically it denotes "original and most basic"; see O'Murchu 1991, 42–49. To appreciate the deeper implications of the vows as being primarily about values see the seminal study of Adrian Van Kaam (1968). Van Kaam uses the term "value radiation" to describe the witness value not just of the vows but of religious life itself for the wider world.

2. In my desire to adopt more inclusive language I use the Greek word *Basileia* (meaning Kingdom) throughout the text to denote what I consider to be the primary biblical and theological foundation for the vowed life as lived by Christians. For further elucidation see O'Murchu 1995, chapter 4.

3. The concept of "liminality" is still relatively new to many readers. Because of detailed explanation in previous works (O'Murchu 1991, 1995), I offer only a brief overview in the present work (see pp. 18ff.) Readers who may wish to explore the wider applications of this concept are referred to Dubisch (1995) for her valuable exposition on the relationship of pilgrimage and liminality; Schwartz-Salant and Stein (1991), who explore its use in therapeutic contexts, and Starkloff (1997), who explores the connection with the church's sacramental life. Although Goehring (1992, 1996) does not use the word "liminality," his research on the marginality of monastic experience uncovers several parallels.

4. Most popular writing on shamanism portrays it as an esoteric, pseudoreligious phenomenon belonging to the ancient past. Its capacity to serve as a prototype for the vowed life is largely unexplored. I first came across the suggestion in Donald Corcoran, "Contemporary Forms of Spirituality and Monastic Life," in Skudlarek 1982, 242–56. In my own work (O'Murchu 1991, 33–36), I draw on the classic study of Mircea Eliade to forge some further links between this ancient practice and the vowed life. Although recent scholars like McNiff and Halifax do not allude to the monastic connection, they surface seminal and original ideas that reinforce many of the ideas explored in this book. See Shaun McNiff, *Art as Medicine* (London: Piatkus, 1992). McNiff's primary concern is healing, which he views as the shaman's primary ability and consequently advises against viewing the shaman as some type of archetypal hero. See also Joan Halifax, *The Fruitful Darkness: Reconnecting with the Body of the Earth* (San Francisco: HarperSanFrancisco, 1993); for Halifax the role of the shaman is to be a power for value radiation. These insights carry immense poten-

tial to undergird the conviction that the vowed life is fundamentally about living nonviolently.

5. I borrow the concept of "value radiation" from Adrian Van Kaam (1968), who applies the concept to the entirety of the vowed life and not just to the vows themselves.

6. The gender question is probably the greatest single and most glaring injustice one encounters in any historical review of the vowed life. Even in a dominant sexist religion like Islam, female religious orders existed in the past, but presently are totally prohibited. Buddhist sisterhoods have fought a long battle for mutual recognition, one that goes on to our own time (see Judy Brink and Joan Mencher, *Mixed Blessings: Gender and Religious Fundamentalism Cross Culturally* [New York and London: Routledge, 1997], 26–39). In Christianity, women always seem to have outnumbered men, and do so today, by three to one, yet, historically the female dimension has been largely subverted. McNamara (1996) has made a courageous attempt at retrieving that subverted tradition.

7. Up until this time, formal Catholic teaching claimed that Christian marriage existed basically for one purpose: the procreation of the species. Since 1962, the official Catholic teaching states that Christian marriage has a dual purpose: (a) the love and intimacy of the spouses for each other; (b) the procreation of the species.

8. Although some schools of organizational management (e.g., the Grubb Institute in London) reserve the use of the term "relatedness" for the functional interaction within organizations, I use the terms "relationships" and "relatedness" interchangeably, each denoting the capacity to relate, the organizational and intimate aspects of which I perceive to be different stages on a continuum rather than two different forms of relating.

9. The belief that humans are innately aggressive or violent owes its origin largely to religion; only in the past hundred years has it been adopted as an anthropological and psychological theory. It is the Freudian influence in particular — which also endorses the "original sin" view of human nature — that enhances this understanding, aggression being understood as a primary instinctual drive. Already in the 1920s, the anthropologist Margaret Mead contested this view and indicated that among the Samoan people the early and liberal introduction to sexual intimacy seemed to reduce considerably people's aggressive drives; this suggestion has been challenged and counterchallenged several times. Also worthy of note is the impressive research of Michael Odent (*The Nature of Birth and Breastfeeding* [London: Bergin & Garvey, 1992]), who associates aggression principally with how babies are treated in the first weeks of life. The most aggressive societies, he notes, tend to separate mother and baby at the moment of birth and refrain from breast-feeding, thus depriving the infant of the more intimate and tactile bonding which breast-feeding fa-

cilitates. Other theorists, notably Arthur Janov (*The New Primal Scream* [London: Abacus Books, 1990]), attribute our "innate" aggression to the violent manner in which modern medicine handles the birth process, often leaving the recipient with a deeply buried sense of primal rage.

10. Ever since the pioneering work of David Bohm, a growing number of contemporary physicists have pursued the relational dynamics at work in the atomic and subatomic worlds. Rarely is attention drawn to the fact that a similar interest can be detected in contemporary biochemistry; for readers of a scientific background I recommend Ronald F. Fox, *Energy and the Evolution of Life* (New York: Freeman, 1988), and Christian de Duve, *Vital Dust: Life as a Cosmic Imperative* (New York: Basic Books, 1995); for those unacquainted with technical jargon, I suggest Michael Crawford and David Marsh, *The Driving Force* (London: Heinemann, 1989), and Beatrice Bruteau, *God's Ecstasy: The Creation of a Self-Creating World* (New York: Crossroad, 1997), esp. 87–138. From a biological perspective, I recommend the many works of Stephen J. Gould or those of Edward O. Wilson.

11. Richard Dawkins is among the main proponents of the "selfish gene" theory, following a rather mechanistic and competitive understanding of Darwin's notion of the survival of the fittest. See his works *The Selfish Gene* (New York: Oxford University Press, 1976), and *The Blind Watchmaker* (London: Penguin, 1990). For an alternative, more altruistic view, see Bruteau 1997, and Crawford 1997. Dawkins, in his most recent work (*Unweaving the Rainbow* [London: Allen Lane / Penguin Books, 1998]), adopts a rather mellowed perspective on issues which he rigidly defended in the earlier works cited above.

Bibliography

Abram, David. 1996. *The Spell of the Sensuous*. New York: Random House.

Bailie, Gil. 1997. *Violence Unveiled*. New York: Crossroad.

Brock, Rita Nakashima. 1992. *Journeys by Heart: A Christology of Erotic Power*. New York: Crossroad.

Brown, Peter. 1988. *The Body and Society: Men, Women and Sexual Renunciation in Early Christianity*. New York: Columbia University Press.

Brueggemann, Walter. 1993. *The Bible and Postmodern Imagination*. Minneapolis: Augsburg Fortress; London: SCM Press.

Bruteau, Beatrice. 1997. *God's Ecstasy: The Creation of a Self-Creating World*. New York: Crossroad.

Burrows, B., A. Mayne, and P. Newbury. 1991. *Into the Twenty-First Century: A Handbook for a Sustainable Future*. London: Adamantine Press.

Chapple, Christopher Key. 1993. *Non-Violence to Animals: Earth and Self in Asian Traditions*. Albany: State University of New York Press.

Chittister, Joan. 1990. *Womanstrength*. New York: Sheed & Ward.

———. 1995. *The Fire in These Ashes*. Kansas City: Sheed & Ward.

Chopp, Rebecca. 1989. *The Power to Speak: Feminism, Language and God*. New York: Crossroad.

Collins, Paul. 1995. *God's Earth*. Melbourne: HarperCollins.

Conlon, James. 1990. *Geo-Justice: A Preferential Option for the Earth*. San Jose, Calif.: Resource Publications.

Crawford, Robert. 1997. *The God/Man/World Triangle: A Dialogue Between Science and Religion*. New York: St. Martin's Press; London: Macmillan.

Daly, Mary. 1973. *Beyond God the Father*. Boston: Beacon Press. New ed., 1985.

———. 1978. *Gyn/Ecology*. Boston: Beacon Press.

———. 1992. *Outercourse*. New York: HarperCollins.

De Dreuille, Mayeul. 1975. *From East to West: Man in Search of the Absolute*. Bangalore: Theological Publications.

Dubisch, Jill. 1995. *In a Different Place: Pilgrimage, Gender and the Politics of a Greek Island*. Princeton, N.J.: Princeton University Press.

Dumezil, George. 1956. *Aspects de la fonction guerrière chez les Indo-Européens*. Paris: Desclée.

——. 1970. *The Destiny of the Warrior*. Chicago: University of Chicago Press.

Dundas, Paul. 1992. *The Jains*. London and New York: Routledge.

Edwards, Denis. 1995. *Jesus the Wisdom of God: An Ecological Theology*. Maryknoll, N.Y.: Orbis Books.

Edwards, Paul, ed. 1976. "Political and Social Theory." *The Encyclopedia of Philosophy*. Vol. 5. New York: Macmillan Publishing Co., 370–87.

Eisler, Riane. 1987. *The Chalice and the Blade*. New York: Harper & Row.

——. 1995. *Sacred Pleasure: Sex, Myth and the Politics of the Body*. New York: HarperCollins.

Evola, Julius. 1983. *The Metaphysics of Sex*. London: East-West Publications.

Ferguson, John. 1975. *The Politics of Love in the New Testament and Non-Violent Revolution*. Cambridge: James Clarke & Co.

Fuller, Reginald and Ilse. 1978. *Essays on the Love Commandment*. Philadelphia: Fortress Press.

Goehring, James E. 1992. "Through a Glass Darkly: Diverse Images of the *apotaktikoi(ai)* of Early Egyptian Monasticism." *Semeia* 58, 28–54.

——. 1996. "Withdrawing from the Desert: Pachomius and the Development of Village Monasticism in Upper Egypt." *Harvard Theological Review* 89, 267–85.

Graham, Elaine. 1995. *Making the Difference: Gender, Personhood and Theology*. London and New York: Mowbray.

Hessel, Dieter T. 1996. *Theology for Earth Community*. Maryknoll, N.Y.: Orbis Books.

Heyward, Carter. 1988. *Our Passion for Justice*. New York: Pilgrim Press.

——. 1989. *Touching Our Strength: The Erotic as Power and the Love of God*. New York: Harper.

Hunt, Mary. 1982. *Fierce Tenderness: A Feminist Theology of Friendship*. New York: Crossroad.

Jaini, Padmanabh S. 1979. *The Jaina Path of Purification*. Los Angeles and London: University of California Press.

Kaku, Michio. 1998. *Visions: How Science Will Revolutionize the 21st Century*. London and New York: Oxford University Press.

Levenson, Jon D. 1985. *Sinai and Zion: An Entry into the Jewish Bible*. San Francisco: Harper & Row.

McFague, Sallie. 1993. *The Body of God: An Ecological Theology*. London: SCM Press.

McNamara, Jo Ann Kay. 1996. *Sisters in Arms: Catholic Nuns through Two Millennia*. Cambridge, Mass.: Harvard University Press.

Miller, William Robert. 1972. *Nonviolence: A Christian Interpretation.* New York: Schocken Books.

Mithen, Steven. 1996. *The Prehistory of Mind.* London and New York: Thames & Hudson.

Moore, Thomas. 1992. *Care of the Soul.* New York: HarperCollins.

———. 1994. *Soulmates.* New York: HarperCollins.

———. 1998. *The Soul of Sex.* New York: HarperCollins.

Morgan, Robin. 1989. *The Demon Lover: On the Sexuality of Terrorism.* London: Methuen.

Nelson, James B., and Sandra P. Longfellow, eds. 1994. *Sexuality and the Sacred.* Louisville: Westminster / John Knox Press.

Nouwen, Henri. 1986. *Reaching Out.* New York: Image Books.

O'Donohue, John. 1997. *Anam Cara: Spiritual Wisdom from the Celtic World.* London and New York: Bantam Press.

O'Murchu, Diarmuid. 1991. *Religious Life: A Prophetic Vision.* Notre Dame, Ind.: Ave Maria Press.

———. 1995. *Reframing Religious Life.* London: St. Paul's Publications.

———. 1997a. *Quantum Theology.* New York: Crossroad.

———. 1997b. *Reclaiming Spirituality.* Dublin: Gill & Macmillan; New York: Crossroad.

O'Shea, Kevin. 1996. *Person in Analysis.* Bristol, Ind.: Wyndham Hall Press.

Plaskow, Judith, and Carol P. Christ. 1989. *Weaving the Vision: New Patterns in Feminist Spirituality.* San Francisco: HarperSanFrancisco.

Raphael, Melissa. 1996. *Thealogy and Embodiment.* Sheffield: Sheffield Academic Press.

Schneiders, Sandra. 1986. *New Wineskins: Re-imagining Religious Life Today.* Mahwah, N.J.: Paulist Press.

Schwartz-Salant, N., and M. Stein. 1991. *Liminality and Transitional Phenomena.* Wilmette, Ill.: Chiron.

Skudlarek, William. 1982. *The Continuing Quest for God: Monastic Spirituality in Tradition and Transition.* Collegeville, Minn.: Liturgical Press.

Starkloff, Carl F. 1997. "Church as Structure and Communitas: Victor Turner and Ecclesiology." *Theological Studies* 58, 643–68.

Tähtinen, Unto. 1976. *Ahimsá: Non-Violence in Indian Tradition.* London: Rider & Co.

Van Kaam, Adrian. 1968. *The Vowed Life.* Denville, N.J.: Dimension Books.

Waldrop, M. M. 1992. *Complexity: The Emerging Science at the Edge of Order and Chaos.* New York: Viking.

Wilshire, Donna. 1994. *Virgin, Mother, Crone: Mysteries of the Triple Goddess.* Rochester, Vt.: Inner Traditions.

The Author: Diarmuid O'Murchu is a member of the Sacred Heart Missionary Congregation, currently ministering in London in a project for homeless people. As a facilitator and consultant he has worked with religious in many countries. His written works include *Religious Life: A Prophetic Vision* (1992), published by Ave Maria Press; and *Quantum Theology* (1997) and *Reclaiming Spirituality* (1998), both published by Crossroad.

ALSO BY

Diarmuid O'Murchu

Quantum Theology
Spiritual Implications of the New Physics

"Pathbreaking — a bold theological map which takes us into
uncharted territory where science, religion, psychology, cosmology,
and spirituality all whirl together in a phantasmagorical dance."
— *Values and Vision*

0-8245-1630-3; $19.95

Reclaiming Spirituality

"In this thought-provoking and rambunctious follow-up to *Quantum
Theology*, O'Murchu celebrates the spiritual renaissance of our time
as an alternative to religious fanaticism and religious indifference."
— *Values and Vision*

0-8245-1723-7; $15.95

Please support your local bookstore, or call 1-800-395-0690.
For a free catalog, please write us at
THE CROSSROAD PUBLISHING COMPANY
370 LEXINGTON AVENUE, NEW YORK, NY 10017

crossroad

OF RELATED INTEREST

—■—

Barbara Fiand, S.N.D.

WRESTLING WITH GOD

Religious Life in Search of Its Soul

"An important book for anyone interested in the shaping of
religious consciousness and spirituality in the context of
contemporary scientific cosmology."
— *Catholic Library World*

"An invitation to religious to bring out into the open
the new ideas they harbor in their hearts."
— *Spiritual Life*

0-8245-1620-6; $14.95

———■———

Please support your local bookstore, or call 1-800-395-0690.
For a free catalog, please write us at
THE CROSSROAD PUBLISHING COMPANY
370 LEXINGTON AVENUE, NEW YORK, NY 10017

We hope you enjoyed
Poverty, Celibacy, and Obedience.
Thank you for reading it.

crossroad